UPDATED & EXPANDED

HEALING TOOLS

*Discover the Keys that Unlock Areas in the Heart
to Release Healing & Freedom*

DR. ANGELA G. WALKER

KINGDOM MEDICINE SERIES VOLUME 2

HEALING TOOLS

© Dr Angela G Walker 2020, 2024
Second Edition
(This is an updated version of the First Edition 'Kingdom Tools' printed in 2020. The title has been renamed 'Healing Tools')

All rights reserved.

No part of this publication may be reproduced or transmitted in any form or by any means, electronic or mechanical, including photocopying, recording or any information storage and retrieval system, without prior permission in writing from the author.

Unless stated otherwise, scripture quotations are taken from the Holy Bible New International Version (NIV) Bible. © 1973, 1978, 1984 by International Bible Society.

Scripture marked 'NASB' are taken from the New American Standard Bible®. Copyright © 1960, 1962, 1963, 1968, 1971, 1972, 1973, 1975, 1977, 1995 by The Lockman Foundation.

Scripture marked 'NKJV' are taken from the New King James Version. Copyright © 1982 by Thomas Nelson, Inc.

Scripture quotations marked 'TPT' are taken from The Passion Translation. Copyright © 2014 by BroadStreet Publishing.

Cover Artist: Rebecca Priestley
Cover Graphics: Caroline Bishop

ISBN: 9798877521919

Acknowledgements

This second edition is an updated and expanded version of the first edition *Kingdom Tools*. The title has been changed to *Healing Tools* because this describes the contents of the book.

I'd like to honour and thank other mature healing ministries for their 'tools' which have contributed in some shape or form to the development of the *Healing Tools* in the *Kingdom Medicine Series*. This includes Dawna Desilva and Teresa Liebscher: *Bethel Sozo Healing Ministries* (www.bethelsozo.com), Reverend Andrew Miller: *HeartSync Ministries* (www.heartsyncministries.org), and Chester and Betsy Kylstra: *Restoring The Foundations* (www.restoringthefoundations.org).

I would like to thank Rachel Gray for editing and proofreading the book, Wendy for her contributions, and for the friends who have provided valuable feedback and comments, especially Guy Rothwell and David King.

Again, I would like to thank Caroline Bishop for her graphic design work on the cover, and Becky Priestly for her prophetic artwork.

DEDICATION

I dedicate this book to the Great Physician, Jehovah-Rapha, from whom we receive spiritual insight and knowledge, wisdom and revelation, counsel and discernment, for every symptom, sickness and disease.

Thank you Heavenly Father, King Jesus and Holy Spirit, for teaching and demonstrating with such love and compassion, grace and mercy, power and authority, wisdom and revelation, how to heal the sick, set the captives free, release the prisoners from darkness, and heal the broken hearted. May all glory, power and honour be Yours, now and forever.

Disclaimers

This ministry does not seek to be in conflict with any medical or psychiatric practice, and values their contribution and input to healing and health care. Rather, it aims to work alongside them, by looking into the possible spiritual and emotional roots to ill health or ongoing symptoms. The ministry aims to connect the natural with the supernatural, and the physical with the emotional and spiritual.

This ministry does not guarantee healing or prevention of symptoms. It facilitates healing and restoration between an individual and God. Hence, the fruits of this ministry will come forth out of the relationship between the person and God. It encourages people to be accountable to others (in the church and medical profession) for their ongoing physical, spiritual, mental and emotional wellbeing.

This ministry is not a substitute for medical advice or medical treatment. It aims to form a bridge between the health services (in hospitals and medical practices), the Christian healing ministries, and the churches.

CONTENTS

Introduction 11
1 Spiritual Hospital 13
2 Battle of the Mind 19
3 Spiritual Discernment 35
4 Power of the Blood 47
5 Curses, Vows & Covenants 61
6 Power of Forgiveness 71
7 Generational Sins & Familial Spirits 85
8 Connecting Our Hearts to Father, Jesus & Holy Spirit . 95
9 Encountering Jesus 113
10 Blessing the Body 123
11 Breaking Soul-Ties 135
12 Overcoming Sexual Issues 141
13 Dealing with Fear & Control 151
14 Unbelief & False Beliefs 171
15 Occult & Free Masonry 179
16 Alternative Medicines 187
17 Prophetic Blessings 205
Conclusion 209
Appendix A: *List of the Occult* 212
Appendix B: *Generational Sins & Curses* 213
Appendix C: *By the Author* 216
Appendix D: *About the Author* 221

Dr Angela Walker did it again! She has compiled what will surely be textbook material for all around health and well being of spirit, soul and body.

Delving deeper in Volume 2 of the Kingdom Medicine Series, Dr Angela goes into the power of the mind, breaking curses, vows and sins, the importance of forgiveness, generational connections, the power of forgiveness, and much more. The importance of addressing these issues is imperative to living lives of triumph.

Not long ago, a medical doctor told a recently diagnosed cancer patient I know to go deal with his unforgiveness issues. Truly the medical field is beginning to realise you can't just treat one's body without addressing the spirit and soul.

Well done to you Angela, and smart are those who devour this important work and live out its contents.

Patricia Bootsma
Catch The Fire Ministries
International Itinerant Speaker
Author of 'Convergence', 'Raising Burning Hearts',' A Lifestyle of Divine Encounters'

Foreword

As Christians, most of us believe that Jesus paid the price for our 'whole' healing. For some there is no problem in believing for physical healing but for some reason believing for 'inner healing' causes some people issues.

I've been a Christian for nearly fifty years but had never come across 'inner healing' until my early fifties. When I understood how much God wanted to free me from long seated soul issues, that's when I finally walked into greater intimacy with the Godhead and freedom, that led me to realising just how much God has for me.

Dr Angela Walker is widely read and researched, as you would expect from someone with her medical background and studies. She has drawn on that medical understanding, widely read diverse Christian writers, and has lived it all while serving in state healthcare hospitals and on the front line multi-culturally as a medical missionary. As more than a well-informed academic, as helpful as they are, these lessons have been learnt, tried and tested in difficult real-life situations.

Dr Walker draws on all of this to produce a comprehensive book, that could almost be used as a manual, that weaves all this together.

Dr Walker's writing recognises that we are all more than just our bodies with thoughts and emotions. We are somehow more than that- we are spiritual. It is hard to find a person that has not prayed at some point in their life.

There is a recognition of the power of timeless truths found in Christian scripture and the biblical practices taught and modelled by Jesus, such as Holy Communion, forgiveness and repentance – both of which set us free from the unhelpful influences and events of our past.

In recent years poor mental health has grown both in its impact and our understanding of its many causes and how it shows up. Dr Walker brings to bear biblical teaching and practices that deal with many of the root causes that keep people trapped personally. She shows how this not only brings personal freedom but will benefit those in relationship with the person fighting these battles.

Her courageous writing is unafraid to "call out" socially acceptable behaviours that create mindsets and habits that keep people tied to, and limited by, their past. There is a passion to empower people to walk free from those events and influences rather than merely learn how to live with them and manage their impact.

While you may not agree with everything you read, I urge you to heed the advice of an old saying – "Don't throw the baby out with the bath water" or a more modern saying "Eat the meat and spit out the bones".

Treat this book like a buffet – it is rich in its diversity and thoughtful, careful preparation. Take what you need for where you are right now – and keep the rest on the back burner, you never know when you or someone you care for will need this nutrition.

Any ministry that facilitates the above is to be celebrated because it not only brings freedom and intimacy but a realisation of just how amazing is God's love for us. He truly wants us to be saved, healed and delivered. That was His heart for us from the beginning. He walked with Adam in the garden....you can't be more intimate than that with our awesome God.

With that in mind, I am pleased to commend Dr Angela Walker's latest book for you to read and to use as you pursue healing for yourself and to facilitate healing for others.

Christine West
Country Facilitator -BETHEL SOZO UK

Introduction

After seven years serving as a medical missionary with Iris Ministries (now called Iris Global) I returned to England and explored the healing tools used in other mature ministries. The combination of these tools along with personal experience and spiritual insights has contributed to the contents of this book.

At the time of releasing the first edition of this book in 2020, the nations were facing a global pandemic crisis caused by the Corona virus, *Covid 19*. The nations were on lockdown to prevent the further spread of this virus. People were facing fears of all kinds as they were ordered to stay at home and socially distance themselves. I believe this was an opportunity to seek God's power to fight the sickness, protect the healthcare workers, overcome the fears, and heal the wounded hearts. Prayer was an essential medicine, if not the most important medicine, during the time of the Corona pandemic.

The purpose of *Healing Tools* is to empower and equip the churches and health workers with various tools for healing the spirit, soul and body. The various tools mentioned in this book are divine keys to help unlock our hearts to receive healing and freedom. These tools can help identify the underlying issues, as well as provide ways to release healing and freedom. Just as there are different departments in a hospital to provide the appropriate medical treatment, so there are various tools to help minister to the emotional, physical and spiritual wellbeing of an individual. However, in order for us to minister effectively with these tools, it requires our hearts to be rooted in a love relationship with God.

One of the purposes to using these tools is to reveal the heart of the Father, Jesus and Holy Spirit, to God's people. There is only one Healer, and His name is Jesus. Our call is to assist Him as we lay down our lives to serve Him. Healing flows in greater measures when our hearts respond with God's heart for those around us.

Jesus said we will be taught by God ourselves (John 6:45). Hence, the more we hang out with God, the more we will learn to hear and discern His voice. We were created for intimacy and the healing anointing flows out of our love relationship with God. Healing plays a significant role in our spiritual growth especially as it enables our hearts to connect with the Father, Son and Holy Spirit.

One of the common areas where we all struggle is the battle of the mind. Our flesh is constantly at war with our spirit, until we learn to recognise and crucify the various aspects of our carnal nature. Some of the main battles we may face daily are fears and false beliefs. One of the ways to overcome our fears, false beliefs and deception, is by seeking His truth and growing in spiritual discernment. As we learn to turn our focus to Him, we will not only discern His ways but discover how to walk in freedom (John 8:32, 14:6).

I have included a chapter on *Alternative Medicines,* not because it is a healing tool, but because many seek healing or become healing therapists by using alternative sources of treatment. As Spirit-filled believers we are to be aware of the spiritual roots and sources of power used in the Complementary Alternative Medicines (CAM's).

My prayer is that the Lord will equip you with the various keys to release healing and freedom in His Kingdom, and may His healing anointing flow in greater measure as you walk in deeper intimacy with Him.

1

Spiritual Hospital

*Praise the Lord, who forgives all you sins
and heals all your diseases*

Psalm 103:3

IN a vision, I saw myself on board a white royal military ship named H.M.S (or His Majesty's Service) and the Captain was King Jesus. The crew were empowered and equipped to rescue captives, free prisoners of war, overcome fears and minister to the wounded. I was taken inside a cabin room which I suddenly realised was a brand-new operating room. On the side was a table with various surgical instruments, neatly displayed on the surface. These were tools used to lance abscesses, remove foreign bodies or skin lesions, cleanse infections and stitch up wounds. I felt familiar with these tools and realised they represented the spiritual tools the Lord had previously given me to do 'minor surgery'. These were the tools to break curses, remove ungodly spirits and cleanse the body from spiritual defilement.

As I looked around, I saw a huge table in the centre. Next, in walked the Great Surgeon, Jesus Himself, and there was a patient lying on the table waiting for an operation. With the patient's consent, He started to operate. When I asked what operation He was performing, He replied, '*Open heart surgery*'. He was cleansing and healing the various parts of the person's heart as well as removing any diseased or non-functioning tissue. When the operation was finished, the person got off the table, completely restored, with a tender loving heart, beating to the same rhythm as His heart beat. The vision ended.

Years later, the Lord reminded me of this ship and I realised there were other rooms, each with their own speciality. Heart surgery was just one of these healing rooms.

Following this vision, it came to mind about the possibility of having a 'spiritual hospital,' where there were various 'spiritual departments' for ministering to the needs of the people. For example, there could be a 'triage' team who refer the 'sick' or 'wounded' to the appropriate people for the relevant ministry. 'Paramedics' are like the healing evangelists who have a passion to deliver ministry and healing on the streets. Some may feel more drawn to minister to the homeless, emotionally wounded, victims in the sex-trade industry, or those suffering with mental illnesses or addictions.

Though the medical profession provides an important part in our physical and general wellbeing, there is still an ongoing need for emotional and spiritual healing in the population today. Hence, this book is to complement the medical profession by providing various keys to unlock hearts to release healing and freedom to the spirit, soul and body.

Here is a suggestive overview for the possible areas of ministry or 'spiritual departments', that could form a 'spiritual hospital' to serve the needs of the people in a local community.

Departments for a Spiritual Hospital in the Community

Hearing God	Worship & Soaking	Blessing the Body	Connecting Hearts to Father, Jesus & HS	Forgive-ness	Encounter Jesus	Power of the Blood
Generat' Sins & Curses	Miscarriage, Abortions & Deaths	Sexual Issues & Soul-ties	Accessing the Courts of Heaven		Divine Heart Surgery	Freeedom from Occult & witchcraft

This suggested overview is not exhaustive and in no particular order, but more of an outline for the possible areas of healing. Most of these shall be discussed in the following chapters. However, *Accessing the Courts, Grief, Addictions, Trauma and Abuse*, will be discussed in Volume Three *Divine Heart Surgery*. Here is a brief overview for each of the above.

Hearing God
Hearing God plays an important part in the healing ministry, both for the recipient and the minister. As we hear God, we can be led by His Spirit how to minister and pray and discern the spiritual or emotional roots to symptoms. Hearing God helps us to hear His truth, and overcome the lies, doubts and fears of the enemy. God's truth is a powerful tool for releasing healing and freedom. (*Hearing God* is discussed in Volume one).

Worship & Soaking
Another way healing can be released is by spending time with God and soaking in His Presence. Soaking can be like marinating in the Spirit as we come before Him, in silence or with worship music. He *restores* our soul especially when we spend time with Him to seek His face and rest in His Presence (Psalm 23:3). Healing may be released through worship, as we focus our eyes and heart on Jesus (Isaiah 6:10).

Blessing the Body
Blessing the body is about honouring our body. It is realizing that our words carry power, whether we choose to curse or bless. There is power in the tongue. Hence, by simply commanding symptoms to leave and speaking blessings instead of curses, we can release healing to the body.

Miscarriages, Abortions & Grief
This is a delicate area for those who have experienced abortions or miscarriages, or are still struggling with grief. As each case is addressed, there can be freedom from grief, death, oppression and depression. (More is discussed in Volume Three.)

Power of Blood & Communion
There is power in the blood of Jesus as it cleanses, heals, protects, breaks curses and ungodly covenants, frees us from ungodly spirits, and redeems us from our sins. Likewise, there is power in the Communion when we take it in a worthy manner. Many are healed and receive divine protection through the sanctifying blood of the Lamb. One of the ways we overcome the enemy is by the blood of the Lamb (Exodus 12:13, Revelation 12:11).

Encountering Jesus
Encountering Jesus is one of the powerful tools used for healing. When Jesus is invited into a wounded memory, such as a fearful or traumatic event, healing is released as the person encounters Jesus and the scene of the memory changes. This is life transforming as the person receives His love, peace and truth in their hearts.

Forgiveness
Forgiveness is a powerful weapon. Some may struggle to forgive themselves, others or God. God doesn't need to be forgiven for He is perfect. However, some have allowed anger or disappointment to come between themselves and God. Forgiveness is a powerful key that unlocks hearts to release healing and also frees us from bondage, especially when we *forgive from the heart* (Matthew 18:35).

Generational Sins & Curses
Generational sins and curses may affect an individual, a group of people, a church or even a nation. The key to freedom is repentance and forgiveness for the sins of our forefathers and this is a powerful weapon to release cleansing and healing. The curses can be broken and reversed with God's blessings for an individual, people group, church or nation (2 Chronicles 7:14).

Accessing the Courts of Heaven
In some situations we may find that ordinary prayer doesn't seem to work and the solution may be to access the Courts of Heaven for further healing, freedom and breakthrough. Accessing the

Courts of Heaven is another powerful weapon or tool, to receive freedom, justice and healing. It is discussed in more detail in Volume three.

Sexual Issues & Soul-ties
When we break ungodly soul-ties from past or present relationships, it releases freedom. As we allow God to heal our hearts from abuse or sexual issues, we will discover our true self and spiritual identity. (Soul-ties and sexual issues are discussed in Chapter 11/12, and healing from the effects of sexual abuse is discussed in Volume three.)

Occult & Freemasonry
Many are bound by ungodly spirits that can inflict ill health and premature death, as a result of past or present involvement with the occult and freemasonry. This may be through direct involvement, or indirectly as a result of generational sins. Addressing each area can release healing and freedom.

Connecting the Heart to Father, Jesus & Holy Spirit
Many of us may struggle in our relationship with Father God, Jesus or Holy Spirit as a result of having previous unhealthy or hurtful relationships with our parents (or parental figures), friends, siblings, or sexual relationships. Through forgiveness and healing, our hearts can be restored and connected to a loving relationship with Father God, Jesus and Holy Spirit.

Divine Heart Surgery
Many may still have wounded areas in their hearts, even after they have forgiven. Divine heart surgery is about engaging in the presence of God, as we assist the Great Surgeon as He gently operates on the wounded and broken areas of the heart. One of the reasons Jesus came was to heal the broken-hearted. (Divine heart surgery is discussed in more detail in Volume three.)

This is an overview of the various healing tools that can contribute to the emotional, physical and spiritual wellbeing of a person, in the churches and communities today.

HEALING TOOLS

2

Battle of the Mind

We demolish arguments and every pretension that sets itself up against the knowledge of God, and we take captive every thought to make it obedient to Christ

2 Corinthians 10:5

The biggest battle we have to face is what goes on between our two ears: the battle of the mind. In fact, enemy strongholds are built on the way we think, be it fear, pride, rebellion, control, unbelief, criticism, insignificance, rejection, and so on. Satan is constantly trying to feed our minds with temptations, distractions, lies, fears or negative thoughts about ourselves, others or God. His mission is to draw us away from intimacy with God and into bondage, as he plans to steal, kill and destroy God's people (John 10:10).

'*The weapons we fight with are not the weapons of the world. On the contrary, they have **divine powers to demolish strongholds**. **We demolish arguments** and **every pretension** that sets itself up **against the knowledge of God** and **we take captive every thought to make it obedient to Christ**'* (2 Corinthians 10:4-5). The Aramaic word used for stronghold can also mean rebellious castle. Paul addressed the strongholds as being 'arguments' or arrogant thoughts, 'pretensions' or deceptions (including deceptive fantasies) that oppose the knowledge of God and mind of Christ. We take captive such thoughts that wage war in our minds between our flesh and spirit, as we surrender each negative (or ungodly) thought to Jesus.

The things we fall victim to are usually the things we believe to be truth when in actual fact they are lies, misperceptions or pretensions from the enemy. All enemy strongholds are based on a lie, false belief or negative thought, hence they distort the way we think and behave. This is known as deception. Satan is the father of lies and deceiver of all things (John 8:44). Negative thoughts are like fiery arrows sent our way, especially during vulnerable and tough times, but can also occur during the more successful moments.

Strongholds have already been touched on in Volume One, but I would like to add this comment by one of the early founders of inner healing, John Sandford. He said this with regards to spiritual strongholds: *'By far the most powerful devices by which Satan controls the minds of his victims are **individual and corporate mental strongholds**. Every living thing God creates has a life and free will of its own. So do our minds. Once we have shaped them, they have a will of their own and do not submit willingly to the will of God, or even to our own wills. **A 'mental stronghold' is a practiced way of thinking that has become ingrained and automatic, with a life and will of its own'**[1]* (Bold print mine). Hence, a mental stronghold is a belief pattern which has become ingrained, and until we take it captive by surrendering it to God, we will not perceive or understand the mind of Christ in this area. Transformation is a process that takes place by the ongoing renewing of our minds (Romans 12:2).

Battle of Flesh and Spirit

Most battles may appear to be of the flesh when the truth is the battle is of the spirit. *'For our struggle is not against flesh and blood, but against the rulers, against the authorities, against the powers of this dark world and against the spiritual forces of evil in the heavenly realms,'* (Ephesians 6:12). We are not meant to get caught up in the demonic realms, but rather learn to overcome by seeing things from God's place of rest, in the heavenly realms. God has raised us up with Christ so we may be seated with Him in the heavenly realms, where all things are placed under His and our feet (Ephesians 1:2-22, 2:6). We come to this place of rest when we surrender our negative thoughts to Jesus in exchange for His peace. Jesus is our Prince of Peace. As we rest in His Presence we have authority to overcome the works of the enemy, because it's the God of *peace* that crushes Satan under our feet (Romans 16:20).

There is an ongoing war between the flesh and spirit, where the enemy can only attack the areas of our flesh we haven't yet surrendered to God. Our body, mind, will and emotions may be telling us one thing, but our spirit may be saying another. God's ways and perspectives are always higher and opposite to the ways we think (Isaiah 55:8). The way to daily renew our minds is by reading His word and engaging our hearts with His Spirit.

I remember a vivid time when my flesh was battling with my spirit. I happened to be in Africa when I received a phone call that my sister was seriously ill in hospital and wasn't responding to treatment. There was a high chance she may die. My friends urged me to go home and be with my parents. My soulish thoughts and emotions made me feel I should return. However, when I prayed, my spirit sensed I was to stay in Africa and it wasn't the right time to return. The interesting thing was when I tried to change my flight, I felt a confusion come on me and couldn't think straight. It was like a daze came over me. In the end, I sensed it was God's will for me to stay and had a deep sense of peace with clarity in my mind and spirit. I knew I had a choice, and chose to trust God with my sister's life. My sister didn't die but made a recovery, and in the meantime, I was able to receive all that God had planned during this significant time of my life in Africa.

Unless our flesh (that is our body and soul), surrenders or comes under the influence of our spirit, then we will be in constant battle with the flesh. Paul said: *'For what I want to do I do not do, but what I hate I do. As it is, it is no longer I myself who do it but it is sin living in me. For what I do is not the good I want to do; no, the evil I do not want to do- this I keep on doing. For in my inner being, I delight in God's law; but I see another law at work in the members of my body, waging war against the law of my mind and making me a prisoner of the law of sin at work within my members,'* (Romans 7:14-24). Paul confessed how he wrestled with his flesh and spirit. His spirit said to do one thing but his flesh opposed. However, he continued by saying this: *'Those who live according to the sinful nature, have their minds set on what that nature desires; but those who live in accordance with the Spirit, have their minds set on what the Spirit desires. The mind of sinful man is death, but the mind controlled by the Spirit is life and peace'* (Romans 8:5-7).

If our spirit is under the influence of the Holy Spirit, then our mind, will and emotions can come under the Lordship of God. Jesus demonstrated this in the desert when He submitted His flesh to His Spirit, and acted from His Spirit at all times. Jesus never responded from His flesh; He always responded from His Spirit. When He heard the distressing news of Lazarus, instead of immediately leaving, He waited. If He had responded from His emotions He would have rushed to the scene, especially when hearing Mary and Martha's anguish, but He didn't. Instead He waited two more days until Lazarus had died. He listened to His Father first and responded from His Spirit. He saw how His Father had other plans.

Jesus told Peter to watch and pray so that he would not fall into temptation. He then said: *'The spirit is willing but the flesh is weak'* (Mark 14:38). As we learn how to pursue His Spirit instead of our flesh, it will become easier to commune with Him and live a Spirit-led life. We were created to be spirit beings and our spirit is to house our physical bodies, not the other way round. This will happen as we daily surrender our flesh to come under the rulership of our spirit, and our spirit to come under the rulership of the Holy Spirit.

The responses made by our flesh are from the orphan areas of our heart. The orphan areas of our heart are the areas we haven't surrendered to Jesus or overcome in the Spirit. Hence, the enemy will keep attacking our flesh until we have surrendered every part to be under the Lordship of Christ. Only then can we truly say that it is no longer I who live but Christ who lives in me (Galatians 2:20). Many still struggle with areas of the flesh simply because they haven't surrendered this area to the Lordship of Christ. Once it is surrendered to Jesus, then the enemy has less power to influence us in this area. This is because the act of yielding to God will disempower the works of the enemy.

Common Battle Grounds [2]

Here are some battles of the mind that we may face daily and once we recognise them, they will become easier to overcome.

Judgment & Criticism
So often, we may unknowingly be judgmental and critical to others or ourselves, especially when we feel hurt, offended, a failure, frustrated, or rejected. Hurt people will hurt other people. People tend to criticise when they feel misunderstood, rejected or disappointed. The problem is each time we think or speak critical words we are opening our hearts to a critical spirit. A critical spirit is based on deceptive enemy language. We are deceived into thinking or feeling we have the right to speak or think such negative thoughts. However, the enemy will use our words to come against us, because the truth is when we judge, we too will be judged (Luke 6:37). Without consciously knowing, we may have come under a spirit of fault-finding, false (or ungodly) judgement and false discernment, especially if we carry a critical-judgemental spirit. The way we overcome is through repenting of such negative thoughts and renouncing the spirits of false-judgement, false discernment, fault-finding and criticism. As we pro-actively guard our hearts and minds from entertaining such negative thoughts (about ourselves, God or others) we will be able to hear and discern God's Spirit.

There was a lady who carried anger, hate, bitterness, jealousy, along with a critical-judgemental spirit in her heart. Her heart had become hardened and resistant to God's Spirit as a result of her negative thoughts and destructive mindset. She attended one of my healing retreats and as her heart became slowly softened she became aware of the judgmental-critical spirit and negative emotions in her heart. The Lord gave me a picture of a flask and I explained that unless we take off the lid, the stuff we harbor in our hearts will remain inside. The lid represented unforgiveness. As we choose to repent of our negative emotions and forgive others, we are removing the lid. Then we can pour out or let go of our toxic thoughts and emotions as we give them to Jesus. However, the vessel still requires cleansing and we cleanse the vessel with the blood of Jesus. Finally, our vessels may be filled with His Spirit. The lady left the retreat with an understanding of how to walk in healing and freedom

One way to renew our minds is with His truth. We can always ask Jesus for His truth and to see others through His lens and from His perspective. This is how we learn to discern His ways and His thoughts, instead of succumbing to the thoughts of our flesh. This is to forgive others or ourselves, for what they, or we, have said, done or not done, and likewise repent where we have entertained a judgemental-critical spirit in our thoughts or words. A judgemental-critical attitude includes fault-finding, accusing others, gossiping, jealous or resentful thoughts, cursing with negative speech or harsh words, and any condemning or intimidating words. When we judge others with an ungodly attitude, we are opening the door of our hearts to the enemy. This is why it is important for those involved in ministry to have clean, compassionate hearts, in order to be open and receptive to His Spirit when ministering to others.

Anxieties & Fears

Many may be held captive or imprisoned by fears and anxious thoughts. This is a daily battle for some until they learn to overcome each anxious thought with His truth. F.E.A.R is False Evidence Appearing Real and anxious thoughts blow things out of proportion to the real truth. Some require inner healing from painful traumas and memories, and others can simply look into Jesus' eyes and hear His words of truth. Some may have had parents who failed to provide protection, security, provision, acceptance or comfort. This then generates fears and anxious thoughts which then produce lies and false beliefs. These can be healed when we choose to forgive those who failed us, and exchange each fear and lie for God's love and truth. We were created to be warriors not worriers. Anxious thoughts are based on false beliefs or fears and we can exchange these for His truth. Jesus will gladly reveal His truth for every anxious thought we surrender to Him, and in exchange give us His peace. He is the source of Truth and Peace (John 14:6, Isaiah 9:6). He said *'Ask and it will be given to you'* (Matthew 7:7). The problem is we are slow to ask Him for His truth. We tend to meditate more on fear and anxiety instead of his word and truth.

Our confidence is not to be in man or ourselves but in Him alone. *'You will keep in perfect peace him whose mind is steadfast, because he trusts in You. Trust in the Lord forever, for the Lord, the Lord, is the Rock eternal'* (Isaiah 26:3-4). His ways aren't our ways and His thoughts aren't our thoughts, because they are far greater than ours (Isaiah 55:8-12). One of the ways we draw closer to Jesus and overcome any anxious thoughts is through prayer and worship. *'The Lord is near. Do not be anxious about anything, but in everything, by prayer and petition, with thanksgiving, present your requests to God. And the peace of God, which transcends all understanding, will guard your hearts and minds in Christ Jesus'* (Philippians 4:6-7). Paul addresses anxiety by first saying 'The Lord is near'. Each time we present our concerns and anxious thoughts to Jesus, we are not to keep hold of them but exchange them for His peace. His peace bypasses our intellect and reaches deep within our hearts. The word used for *guard* is a military word because His peace guards or protects our hearts and minds. Cast all your anxiety on Him, for He cares for you (1 Peter 5:7).

There was a season in my life when I had no idea what I was going to be doing next or where I would be living. I struggled with fear and anxious thoughts about my future for I felt I had no control. Each time I received prayer, the Lord would ask me to give Him the control reins and did I trust Him with my future. For a short period I would feel His peace in my heart and be at rest, until my mind battled again with the fear and anxious thoughts. This was a battle I gradually overcame as I chose to put my faith and trust in God, and realised the truth that my life was in His hands.

Vanity & Pride
God created us to be significant, accepted, valued, loved and to belong. However, as a result of our childhood experiences, some may feel unloved, ignored, not listened to, rejected or insignificant. Consciously or subconsciously, we feel the need to achieve, belong, and feel significant, as a result of our orphan

heart. Subsequently, these thoughts may develop into a form of vanity or pride.

On our own, we can do little in God's Kingdom, but with God we get to do the outrageous, extraordinary and most amazing things. Jesus gives grace to the humble but opposes the proud (1 Peter 5:5). His grace is the supernatural power and ability to do what we can't do in our own natural strength. The Lord knows the motives of our hearts, for nothing is hidden from Him. However, He rewards those who pursue Him: '"*Let him who boasts **boast in the Lord**." For it is not the one who commends himself who is approved, but the **one whom the Lord commends**,*' (2 Corinthians 10:18).

We all fall short of pride to some degree or other. Pride is where we think more of ourselves than others. The middle letter of pride is 'I' and self-focus is an orphan area of our hearts. Some may have pride of knowledge, pride of religion, pride of upbringing or who they know, pride of achievement, pride of possessions, and so on. Self-pity is a form of pride as is self-righteousness. Self-pity is where we are in the pit of self, and self-righteousness is where we always think we are right or better than others. One way to humble ourselves is to daily surrender our hearts (mind, will and emotion) to Jesus and seek His will and thoughts above our own. A sense of freedom and peace is received in our hearts when we choose to follow Him.

Distractions & Temptations

Many times, we may fail to recognize the distractions and temptations of the world, flesh and devil, which are contrary to the Spirit and will of God. It is easy to be distracted with food, pleasures, and things that feed our flesh. John highlights this: '*Do not love the world or anything in the world. For everything in the world- the **cravings of sinful man, the lust of his eyes and the boastings of what he has and does** – comes not from the Father but from the world,*' (1 John 2:15-17). Even in ministry, some may crave after success, fame, or lust for wealth, or to elevate themselves above others. Though we are in the world, we do not belong to the world (John 15:19).

When the Lord calls us to press in deeper with Him, or to fast and pray, our flesh tries to resist. This is because we easily give into tiredness or the needs of the flesh, instead of focusing our spirit on Jesus. When the Lord asked the disciples to stay awake and pray, they gave into their flesh and tiredness, and fell asleep. In the same way, we are to stay awake so we don't fall into temptation. He said: *'Watch and pray so that you will not fall into temptation. The spirit is willing but the flesh is weak,'* (Matthew 26:40-41).

One of the ways to overcome temptations is to daily surrender our entire being to Him, by offering our body, soul and spirit to Him as a living sacrifice (Romans 12:1). We can choose to depend on His grace to do what He has called us to do, instead of striving with our flesh or natural abilities. As we regularly pray in tongues (whether silently or aloud) this will enable our spirit to stay alert to the promptings of His Spirit (Eph 6:18).

Sometimes, the Lord may prompt us to fast. It may be a fast from food or a non-food fast. Fasting involves laying aside the desires of the world (including social-media) and flesh so we may hunger for more of His Presence and Spirit. The enemy attempts to draw our hearts away from God through distractions and temptations, whereas prayer and fasting draws our hearts back in alignment with God's Spirit.

What is Deception?

One of the battles of the mind is the area of deception. Deception means being tricked or misled, or made to believe in something that is false. We are all deceived beings, some more than others. It is easy to fall into deception when we are misguided by other people's thoughts or advice. Most of the time, we are unaware of being deceived until the truth comes to light and exposes the deception or lie. Hence deceptive thoughts can easily lead us into captivity or imprisonment.

John said if we claim or think we are without sin, then we are *deceived*, and God's *truth* isn't in us (1 John 1:8). One of the enemy's main weapons is deception. He is out to hold back the truth and keep us in bondage as long as he can. Our minds are held captive until the Holy Spirit reveals the truth. Jesus is the Truth and He sent His Spirit of Truth to lead us into freedom (John 14:6+17). It is His Truth that sets us free from bondage (John 8:32). I have seen many people walk in freedom once they realise the truth concerning a situation or the way God sees them.

The more we become aware of the enemy's weapons and schemes, the less likely we will be imprisoned by his lies and deception. Self-pity is a good example of where he deceives us. He invites us to throw pity parties when things don't work out for us. As we do, we walk into a pit of self that turns us away from God. The Lord showed me how self-pity is a sin. The moment I realised this, I repented and renounced the spirit of self-pity. I don't entertain it anymore, since I know where it is from.

Another area where we easily fall into deception is thinking life is about striving for success and achievement. This is a worldly concept and not of the Kingdom. It is from the orphan heart, that is, the part of our carnal nature that hasn't connected to the heart of God. As a result, we strive for achievement with our natural abilities, until God speaks His truth. We were created to have intimacy with Him. Our relationship with Him matters more to Him than what we do for Him. He actually wants to crucify our worldly need for success and achievement. Life is not about how big I can make my ministry or empire, or how successful I become, but what effect I can have to help others grow in their relationship with God. Success is to be measured by God's standards and not man's, for success is about having an intimate relationship with God as we pursue His Spirit. We succeed not by might nor by power but by His Spirit abiding in us (Zechariah 4:6). This refers to overcoming the ways of the world through the seven-fold Spirit: *His Spirit of Wisdom, Knowledge, Revelation, Counsel, Power, and Fear of the Lord* by choosing a lifestyle of abiding in His Presence (Isaiah 11:2).

Western culture is very work focused and I was brought up to believe life was about achievement and success. However, the Kingdom of God is not work focused but people and relationship focused. Hence the first two commandments are *love the Lord your God...and love your neighbour* as yourself (Luke 10:27).

When we repeatedly struggle with the same thing, it may be because we have developed an ungodly stronghold. It is good if we can recognize and deal with this. The enemy tries hard to keep us from knowing the truth. He wants us to believe the lie that 'this is the way we are' or 'this is the way we have to live our lives' or 'we are in the right and others are wrong'. Jesus came to break these lies and set our minds free with His Spirit of truth, for where the Spirit of God is there is freedom (2 Corinthians 3:17).

I saw a woman who was struggling to forgive her best friend who had let her down. The issue was she had set standards which her friend couldn't live up to. She felt disappointed with the friendship and expected far more than she got. As we prayed, she was able to forgive her friend and the Lord shone His truth on the situation. She realised how she had been deceived about friendship. The only person who would never let her down was Jesus. He was to be her best friend. And from her relationship with Jesus she could learn how to love others. She learnt the truth that we can't own or possess or try to control anyone. Friendship is to be based on unconditional love, not what you can get out of it. Many truths were revealed as the Lord began to heal this area of her orphan heart.

One of the reasons we become easily deceived is that we don't seek God's truth or perspective on things. We rely too much on the voice of the flesh, false beliefs or the ways of the world. The wisdom of the world is foolish compared to God's Wisdom, and the foolishness of God is wiser than man's wisdom. Jesus is Wisdom personified (1 Corinthians 1:25 +30, 3:18). The more we learn how to hear God, the more we will discover His truth and be set free from different areas of deception. Jesus said: *'My sheep listen to My voice; I know them, and they follow Me,'* (John 10:27-28).

The only one who is without deception is the one who walks one hundred percent with God and is without sin. Jesus is the only one I know who qualifies for this. Until we deal with the various areas of sin in our life, we too are living in deception.

John said: *'If we claim to be without sin,* **we deceive ourselves and the truth is not in us. If we claim we have not sinned, we make Him out to be a liar and His word has no place in** our lives,' (1 John 1:8-10). The good news is we discover more of His truth as we follow Him and walk in His ways. We are all on a life long journey that leads to healing, wholeness and inner freedom. We can choose what lens we look through, and ask God to see things through His lens. When we look through God's lens, we will be able to see and discern with more clarity, instead of with a blurred vision. Jesus has sent us His Spirit of truth (John 15:26).

Paul lived in deception before his encounter with Jesus. After this, he was on the path of discovering the truth as he followed God and discerned His ways. When Paul wrote to the Romans, Corinthians, Ephesians, Thessalonians, Galatians, Timothy and Titus, he constantly referred to the deception in the world and warned them not to be influenced by the deceivers (Romans 16:18; 1 Corinthians 3:18, 15:33; 2 Corinthians 6:8; Galatians 6:3; Ephesians 4:14, 5:6; 2 Thessalonians 5:3; 2 Timothy 3:13; Titus 1:10). Likewise, John the Beloved knew the truth because he remained close to the heart of Jesus. He also addressed the area of deception in many of his writings (John 7:12, 8:44; 1 John 1:8, 3:7; 2 John 7; Revelation 20:3 ,8,10). Let us be those who are seekers and discerners of His ways and truth.

Two Wisdoms

Many of us may battle with the flesh and spirit through a lack of wisdom and discernment. There are two wisdoms; the wisdom of the world and the Wisdom of God. The Wisdom of the Lord brings peace, truth and freedom, whereas the wisdom of the world brings fear and bondage. The Wisdom of God comes from the Tree of Life (Proverbs 3:18), whereas the wisdom of this world comes from the Tree of Knowledge of Good and Evil.

Jesus is the Wisdom of God (1 Corinthians 1:30). He is the Way, the Truth, the Word and the Life. True Wisdom always focuses on God and His people (Matthew 11:19, Proverbs 8:12-14). However, the wisdom of the world is focused on 'self' since it comes from the world, flesh and devil. It comes from the mindset of man instead of God. Human or worldly wisdom is deceptive, though it appears to be real. It will stop us fulfilling our call and destiny for it is based on fears, false beliefs, insecurities and man's thoughts, instead of God's thoughts.

I believe Adam and Eve were originally spirit beings, radiating His light and glory as they ate from the Tree of Life. However, the moment they ate from the Tree of Knowledge of Good and Evil, they lost their garment of light and immortality. At that point, they became aware they had flesh for they were now mortal beings. They became mortal as a result of focusing on the wisdom of the world, which was from the Tree of Knowledge of Good and Evil. Not everything that is good is from God, as we see in the case of the things from the Tree of Knowledge of *Good* and Evil. The enemy can deceive us to believe things are good to draw our hearts away from God, as he did with Adam and Eve.

One of the things for us to discern is the difference between the wisdom of the world and the Wisdom of God. The Wisdom of God is Jesus Himself, and points to His ways and His Spirit. This is contrary to the wisdom of the world which points to 'self' and the flesh.

Now there is the *gift* of wisdom and the *Spirit* of Wisdom. The gift of wisdom is one of the gifts of the Spirit Paul speaks about and is available for everyone (1 Corinthians 12:8). James said: *'If any of you lacks wisdom, he should ask God, who gives generously to all'* (James 1:5). We ask by faith for God is a generous giver and wants His children to see through His eyes of Wisdom, instead of the wisdom of this world. However, the Spirit of Wisdom is one of seven-fold Spirits that is seen in those who carry His Presence and revere His Name (Isaiah 11:2). Daniel was a mature son of God, who reverently feared God's holy Name. He carried such humility and a servant heart, never seeking after any reward, but always worshipping God and praising Him. He was willing to lay down his life for the Lord, instead of fearing man or worshipping other gods. Hence, God gave him His Wisdom and Revelation to interpret dreams, visions and riddles that no-one else could do, because Daniel feared the Lord and his heart was totally surrendered to Him (Daniel 2:20-23).

The Lord will give His Wisdom to those who ask in a time of need. However, the Spirit of Wisdom is given to those who live a life of complete submission to the Lord, reverently fearing His Name and abiding in His Presence.

Dealing with Disappointment

Many, if not all of us, have probably faced disappointment at some point in life. This can range from minor to major, depending on how quickly we deal with it or get over it. We can be disappointed with ourselves, others or God, especially when things don't turn out the way we want or expect. It is easier to blame God or others for our disappointments, when the truth may be that we are to take ownership for our negative thoughts.

Dis-appointment with God means not being in 'appointment' or alignment with Him. To put it another way, it is when we step out of line with His will. We can ask God to reveal His truth concerning each situation, so we see from His perspective instead of our own or the enemy's perspective. This will bring comfort, healing and freedom from any past or present disappointments.

I felt disappointed with God when things didn't turn out as I had expected during my gap year. I felt God had let me down, and as a result I chose to walk away from Him. I blamed Him for leaving me, as I felt alone and abandoned. One day as I poured out my heart to Him, I asked, *'Why did You leave me God?'* Suddenly, as I lay down in a field, His Glory-Presence came upon me. I felt overwhelmed by His majestic Presence and He said: *'Ange, I didn't leave you. You left Me.'* I felt such unconditional love along with an inner conviction as I was made aware of this truth. I realised how the enemy had tricked me. The truth was I had stepped out of His will. Where I felt He had let me down, He hadn't. I was simply not in alignment with His will. As I instantly repented, my spirit was connected back to His Spirit. It felt like I was back on the path where I had left Him.

There was another time I felt hugely disappointed with God when I failed one of my final medical exams. There was no reason I should have failed, for I had studied hard and I knew He had called me to be a doctor. However, I had to deal with this feeling of disappointment towards Him. So I cried out to Him, venting all my frustration and anger, and asked why He let me fail. After releasing my negative emotions, He replied to my spirit. He said it was because I had allowed pride to enter my heart, and reminded me that I would succeed not by might or by strength but by His

Spirit. When I realised this, I instantly repented and humbled myself, and His peace flooded my heart again. Six months later, I re-sat the exam and walked through it no problem. It dawned on me that the real test I had to pass was the test of my heart.

If we give our *dis*-appointments to God, and let go of our negative emotions and frustrations, He will come and reveal His truth. When we see things from His perspective and hear His voice, everything falls into place and the disappointment goes.

I saw a lady who felt a disappointment with God after her husband walked out with her children. She cried out to God, and asked Him why did He not intervene and stop her husband from leaving? After she released tears of deep pain, I saw in my spirit Jesus standing by her. So I asked her to look into His eyes. As she gazed into His eyes of suffering love, her tears soon turned into laughter and joy. She felt His warm liquid love flooding through her innermost being. She soon realized He had never left her and had always been with her. The Lord said: *'Those who hope in Me will not be disappointed'* (Isaiah 49:23). As we trust in God and look to Him, He will never disappoint us.

Declare His Truth & Promises

One of the ways to overcome the battles of our mind is to *take captive every thought and make it obedient to Christ* (2 Corinthians 10:5). This sounds easy but we are to be aware of our negative thoughts in order to resist them and take authority over them. Paul said we are to be transformed by the renewing of our minds (Romans 12:2). The word 'renewing' refers to an ongoing process, meaning a continual renewal of the way we think, until our minds become more transformed into the likeness of Christ.

In a vision, I saw a person walking along a path and this was the path of Life. Suddenly, fog appeared and the path was no longer visible. The person became confused for they could no longer see where they were going. However, they could either walk through this fog which represented uncertainty, confusion or doubt, with the risk of veering from the path, or they could ask the Lord to make the path visible through their spiritual eyes. Their minds were to rise above the doubt and confusion, so they could see with clarity through the eyes of faith. As we choose to focus on the Spirit, His word will become a light to our path (Psalm 119:105). Paul asked the Father to give us His Spirit of Wisdom and Revelation, so that the *eyes of our heart* may be enlightened, to know the hope to which He has called us (Ephesians 1:17-18).

There have been seasons in my life when it has been difficult to see where I was going or know what God was doing. Many times I have felt tempted to quit and return to my former work. It has been like climbing a spiritual mountain and at various points tempted to turn back instead of continuing on up. However, I managed to continue on up with the help of others encouraging me with God's words and promises. In hindsight, I realised it was during these seasons that my heart and spirit were being tested. God was taking me deeper in Him, though at the time it felt like He was miles away.

Sometimes, we are to stand on His truth and declare His word and promises, as we walk through such seasons of uncertainty. When we declare His word, truth and promises, things may begin to stir in the heavenly realms, and this can bring a breakthrough in our lives on earth. Declaring His word, truth and promises is more powerful than rehearsing negative words or doubtful thoughts. As we rise in the Spirit, declare in the Spirit, see in the Spirit, then we will overcome in the Spirit, even when things look doubtful or impossible. God is God of the impossible. We just need to believe and declare it, as we choose to walk by faith instead of by our natural sight (2 Corinthians 5:7).

The battle of the mind becomes easier as we learn to take ownership for our negative thoughts and yield them to Jesus. He is the source of all peace and truth and will give this in exchange for all fears, false beliefs, and ungodly thoughts we yield to Him.

END NOTES:

[1] Sandford, John; *Healing the Nations (Chosen Books, 2000), p 151*
[2] Meyer, Joyce; *Battlefield of the mind*
  Joyner, Rick; *Epic Battles of the Last Days; The Final Quest*
  Jackson, Harry R; *The Warrior's Heart*

3

Spiritual Discernment

*Dear friends, do not believe every spirit, but
test the spirits to see whether they are from God*

1 John 4:1

Spiritual discernment is something we all need, especially during the times we are living in. It is a valuable tool in ministry and can be acquired either as a gift or a fruit of the Spirit. The man without the Spirit doesn't accept the things that come from the Spirit of God, because they are *spiritually discerned* (1 Corinthians 2:14). Those who walk with the Lord learn to discern His ways and distinguish His thoughts from the thoughts of man and the enemy.

When God told Solomon he may have whatever he wanted, Solomon asked for a *discerning heart* so he may govern God's people and discern right from wrong (1 Kings 3:9). God gave him the gift of discernment and he was known as the wisest of all kings. Paul refers to the *discernment of spirits* as one of the nine spiritual gifts (1 Corinthians 12:10). Some translations refer to this as 'distinguishing between the spirits' (NIV) and others refer to it as the ability to 'discern the source', that is, whether a word is from the Holy Spirit, human (flesh) or demonic origin (TPT).

All thoughts, feelings and words come from a source. The source can either be from the flesh (including the world), the devil or God. Jesus said His sheep know His voice for they have become accustomed to hearing Him. We develop an ability to *generally discern* between what is of God and what isn't as we mature in our spiritual growth and sonship (Hebrews 5:14).

General Discernment

The word *discern* used in the Old Testament is the ability to distinguish between good and evil. When King Solomon asked God for a discerning heart, he said: *'So give Your servant a **discerning heart** to govern Your people and to **distinguish between right and wrong**'* (1 Kings 3:9). Paul said the man without the Spirit of God doesn't accept the things that come from the Spirit of God and cannot understand them for they are *spiritually discerned* (1 Corinthians 2:14). Hence, we require the Spirit of God in our hearts in order to distinguish what is from God and what isn't.

General discernment comes with experience and maturity: *'Solid food is for the mature, **who by constant use have trained themselves to distinguish good from evil**'*. The New American Standard version reads: *'Have **their sensors trained to discern good and evil**'* (Hebrews 5:14).

Spiritual discernment comes with maturity as we grow more in our relationship with God. Many may say, 'God is speaking', but we are to test this for ourselves. Jesus warned there will be false prophets and anti-Christs, and not to believe what they say. *'At that time if anyone says to you, "Look, here is the Christ!" or "There he is!" do not believe it. For false Christs and false prophets will appear and perform great signs and miracles to deceive even the elect- if that were possible. See, I have told you ahead of time'* (Mathew 24:23-25).

There will be those who come and perform miracles, signs and wonders, and our role is to discern if their source of power is from God or not. *'And he (the beast) performed great and miraculous signs, even causing fire to come down from Heaven...**he deceived the inhabitants** of the earth'* (Revelation 13:13, 2 Thessalonians 2:9).

Sometimes, fellow believers who mean to speak well are not necessary speaking from the heart of God, but their flesh. We are to test what we hear (even from those who have a prophetic anointing) for they may not always be speaking from God's heart.

Nehemiah was given 'ungodly wisdom' and intimidating words from a prophet who falsely prophesied he would be killed if he didn't flee from his work. He discerned where these words were coming from and rejected them, for they were not from God (Nehemiah 6:10-14). This highlights for us to be careful not to assume what someone says is from God, even if they say it is, without checking it out with God first.

Paul encourages us to '*test everything*' we hear so that we can hold onto the good, or that which is from God, and discard the evil. There are many believers who quench what the Holy Spirit is doing by rejecting what they see or hear when actually it is from God. We simply can ask God, '*Is this really You, Lord?*' Paul tells us not to quench the Spirit's fire or treat prophecies with contempt (1 Thessalonians 5:19-22). John, on the other hand, encourages us not to believe every spirit we hear, but to test the spirits to see whether they are from God or not. Many may come and give a false prophesy, hence we are to discern if the word is from God (1 John 4:1-2, 2 Thessalonians 2:9).

I have come to understand that when someone has given me a true prophetic word from God, or speaks under the power of the Holy Spirit, I usually feel a stirring in my spirit that is good and brings life. It is as if my spirit becomes alive or feels on fire, or I may feel the joy, love or peace of the Holy Spirit inside me. When Jesus spoke to the disciples on the road to Emmaus, their hearts burned within. However, when a word given to me is not from God, I usually notice my spirit doesn't respond. Instead, it washes over me or I may feel a heaviness and loss of peace within. If it washes over me, then it is usually from the flesh, but if my spirit feels heavy or not at peace, then it is usually from the enemy. Jesus said: '*The **Spirit** gives life; the **flesh** counts for nothing. The words I have spoken to you are **Spirit** and they **are life**'* (John 6:63).

However, I would also like to mention there have been occasions when a word or prophecy has been spoken in my life that has been of God but my spirit hasn't responded, for I have not been in the right place with God at that moment in time or my heart didn't want to receive this word. So we are to be careful not to discard the words that don't automatically bring life to our spirit but test them before God, especially if it is a word involving significant change.

I received a prophetic word spoken by a man of God and my spirit didn't respond for the word didn't make sense. But on further discussion with others and testing it before God, my spirit became more open to hear what God was trying to tell me.

On another occasion there were two pastors with prophetic gifting who had spoken significant words in my life. One was strongly encouraging me to do one thing and the other was strongly telling me the opposite. So I got before God in prayer and fasting to seek His will on the matter. After a few hours of laying down my concerns and waiting on Him, I felt a deep peace on what choice to make. His still quiet voice spoke to my spirit as I engaged in His Presence. He made His will clear by revealing who was speaking from the flesh.

God wants us to bring everything to Him so we can hear and obey His voice. We are to test everything we hear by bringing it before God and not assuming it is from Him because of the person who spoke the word. When people hear me speak or teach about things that they haven't heard before, I will encourage them to ask the Lord what He says and to seek His truth on the matter.

Discerning the Spirit from the Flesh
It is good to discern between the flesh (body and soul) and spirit because there is a constant battle going on between the two. Our body, mind, will or emotions may be telling us one thing but our spirit may be telling us another. The soul feeds from the Tree of Knowledge of Good and Evil, whereas the spirit feeds from the Tree of Life.

One day, as I was praying for some church leaders, I had a picture. In the picture, I saw one of the pastors on his knees in prayer listening to God with streams flowing in all directions from his heart. As he came before God, he was tapping into the Tree of Life. Hence, the River of Life was flowing in all directions from his heart as he focused on God. However, to his left I saw the Tree of Knowledge of Good and Evil. It was trying to distract him by 'good' man-made suggestions and ideas that were not from God. The pastor couldn't afford to agree with these man-made suggestions, for they would quench the flow of the Spirit. They were counterfeit to God's Spirit. Hence, all thoughts and suggestions were to be 'tested' by offering them to God in prayer. For example, someone had suggested how 'good' it would be to have stage smoke for a youth church service. This was easy to produce and a copy of something real, but it was man-made smoke. The Lord can provide His manifest Presence, His cloud of glory, if we are willing to seek Him and engage in His Presence. It will come. Do we settle for what is counterfeit from the Tree of Knowledge of Good and Evil, or pursue what is authentic and real from the Tree of Life?

I believe we are to be led by our spirit and not our flesh. Jesus demonstrated this in the desert when He submitted His flesh to His Spirit, and acted from His Spirit at all times. When we pray and come into God's Presence, it is easier to respond from our spirit. Hence, as we regularly interact with God, our spirit will begin to take rule over our flesh. Let's not forget, we were created to be spiritual beings residing in physical bodies.

Check the Motive
Whenever we receive a prophetic word or 'good' suggestion or proposal, it is good to check the underlying motive behind the source. Are the motives pure and sincere, flowing from the Tree of Life? Or are they contrived with an ulterior motive coming from the Tree of Knowledge of Good and Evil? Here are some thoughts to help to discern.

Tree of Knowledge of Good and Evil
Is the person who is giving the word displaying any greed, selfishness, personal bias, jealousy, pride, fear or control? Are they seeking anything for themselves or do they have the individual's best interests at heart? Check the motive behind the word and that will help confirm the source of where it is coming from. People have said God was speaking a certain word to me, but when I have sensed any fear, control, the flesh, 'good ideas' or ungodly spirits, I have graciously not accepted it.

Solomon checked the motive behind two women's testimony when they both claimed that a baby was theirs. He tested their hearts by seeing which one would stop him from cutting the baby in half. Then he knew who was the real mother, for her motives were genuine and loving (1 Kings 3:16-27). The Lord searches our hearts and knows every motive behind our thoughts.

Tree of Life
A word spoken from the Tree of Life comes with unconditional love, selflessness and humility. The word will point to God and not self. The word may come through dreams, visions, or spiritual insights during prayer or worship. The word can be outrageous and something never imagined, or like a light suddenly turned on. You clearly know it is not your own thought for the idea is God focused and comes by revelation of the Spirit. It is usually amazing for it requires radical faith and obedience, since it is 'out of the box' thinking. There is no place for 'self' for it is God's idea because it is revelatory. It causes the spirit to come alive and feel excited. It stirs faith and requires more prayer and leaning on God for strategy, counsel and wisdom. It can't be done by the flesh but requires God's grace and Wisdom. And this means we are to trust in Him because He is in charge. His peace rests with us when our confidence isn't in self or others, but Him. Kingdom Wisdom is full of revelation and focused on Jesus, and is contrary to the world's thinking.

Is it possible for the same Christian to speak a word from God one moment and then a word from the flesh or devil the next moment? Yes! No-one is perfect and we are all prone to sin. This means we are to weigh up what we hear for ourselves and whether it is from God or not. This was seen with Peter, when Jesus asked Peter, *'Who do you say I am?'* Peter replied He was the Christ, the Son of the living God. Jesus blessed Peter and said this revelation was given to him by his Heavenly Father. However, a few verses later when Jesus told His disciples He must suffer and be killed, Peter rebuked Jesus by saying: *'This shall never happen to You!'* Jesus replied: *'Get thee behind Me Satan! You are a stumbling block to Me'* (Mathew 16:15,23). A similar thing happened with James and John, when they were not welcomed in a Samaritan village. They asked Jesus if they should call fire down from Heaven and destroy the village. Jesus rebuked them and they continued on their journey (Luke 9:51-55). Peter, James and John, whom Jesus rebuked, were His closest disciples.

When we lack discernment, we are at greater risk of falling into deception. However, as we seek God by yielding our flesh to His Spirit, we will learn to discern His ways.

Is it from the Flesh, Devil or God?

Here are some ways to help us discern if the source of what we think, feel, see or hear is from the flesh (or world), the devil or from God. As we draw closer to God, we will become more familiar with the ways He speaks, for His sheep know His voice (John 10:4).

Source from the Flesh
'We have not received the spirit of the world, but the Spirit who is from God, that we may understand what God has freely given us. We speak not in words taught us by **human wisdom but in words taught by the Spirit***, expressing* **spiritual truths in spiritual words***. The man* **without the Spirit does not accept the things that come from the Spirit of God***, for they are foolishness to him, and he can't understand them for they are spiritually discerned***...For the wisdom of this world is foolishness in God's sight'* (1 Corinthians 2:12-14, 3:19). People who lack the Spirit of God will not accept the things which are from God. This is important to recognise so we are not swayed by worldly or man-made opinions.

'See to it that no-one takes you captive through hollow and deceptive philosophy which depends on human tradition and the basic principles of this world rather than on Christ' (Colossians 2:8). Most of the traditions or cultures of this world are man-made and not God-made. Jesus told us to focus on His Kingdom by seeking first the Kingdom of God and His righteousness (Mathew 6:33).

When a word or thought is from the flesh it is usually based on man-made logic, common sense, reasoning and self-opinion. If there is any fear, anxiety, guilt, doubt, anger, criticism, jealousy, pressure or other negative feelings behind it, then it probably is from the flesh or enemy. If there is a sense of any fear or control behind someone's 'wise' words, then they are probably not from

God. Human wisdom sees things from God as foolish, for it sees things as the world sees.

Also, things of the flesh will feed our flesh especially in the areas of greed, possessions, wealth, comfort, pride, and the lust for power, fame or status. The flesh is self-focused instead of God-focused, and follows traditional beliefs instead of a Kingdom culture. Since the flesh opposes the word of God, our spirit will lack any response.

Source from the Devil

The devil is cunning and deceptive for he never wants us to know our words or thoughts are from him. As we recognize the devil's schemes and character we will discern when things are from him.

One of his traits is to accuse others, since he is the accuser of the brethren (Zechariah 3:1). We are to do away with the pointing finger and malicious talk or gossip (Isaiah 58:9). Any accusations, even if true, are not from God but the devil. This is because God convicts but the enemy condemns. Instead of accusing others we are to forgive and point them in the right direction through love.

The enemy condemns by bringing judgment and makes you feel there is no way out. Jesus, on the other hand, convicts by speaking the truth in love and offers us a solution or way out through forgiveness and the cross. *'God didn't send His Son into the world to condemn the world, but to save the world through Him'* (John 3:17). We have only one true Judge and that is God (James 4:12).

A word or thought from the enemy is usually negative, fearful or self-focused. It can bring a sense of guilt, shame, hopelessness and despair. Also, there may be a sense of failure and disappointment. It releases doubt instead of faith. Ungodly words release a sense of unease or oppression.

Since Satan is the father of lies, the thought may be a lie or a twist in the truth. If the source isn't of God then we reject it. He will deceive us into believing a sin is ok (Jude 4). There are no excuses for any sin. Sin is sin.

Sometimes, the word or thought can come with pride of knowledge, self-righteousness, 'my rights' or a sense of superiority to others. The thought may be glorifying self instead of glorifying God. Hence, we are to recognise the words of flattery and the praises from men, because they are usually not from God (John 12:43). This is not to be confused with words of encouragement given by others that are usually a blessing.

In other cases, there may be a sense of pressure or manipulation to do something against personal will. Words spoken in a manipulative or controlling manner usually come from a source of witchcraft.

Thoughts from the enemy are opposite to the character and nature of God. Such thoughts do not bear Kingdom fruit. Hence there will be no peace, joy, love, self-control, gentleness, humility and so on. Or the word may sound good but be coming from an ungodly source. There is usually no peace and something just doesn't feel right. I have met people who know how to say the 'right words', but then noticed there was an underlying spirit of fear, manipulation, people pleasing, or pride.

Also, words not from God can bring confusion and lack clarity, or may come with oppression. Sometimes, we may feel a sense of false guilt or false responsibility. This is when we are made to feel guilty or responsible for something which was not our problem in the first place. People usually blame others when it is their own fault. The spirit of fault-finding is not from God. The closer we draw near to God, we will come to know His ways and discern what is of the enemy and what is of Him.

The enemy usually tempts us to do things we shouldn't whereas God invites us to follow and obey Him. After I had finished a locum job as a Consultant Paediatrician, I was tempted with words of praise and flattery from colleagues to take on another job in the same department. As I was thinking about it, the Holy Spirit convicted me of my motives. Pride was the motive to accept the job and then I sensed it wasn't God's will. So I resisted the temptation and turned the job down. God had something far better planned for me and it was the beginning of an adventure with Him.

Source from God
Sometimes, things may happen in life that seem to be from the enemy, but may be from God. We are to ask God if He is behind what is happening or if it is an attack from the enemy. However, it

may be the enemy has initiated something, but with prayer, God can work in it for the good. Sometimes, God may use a negative experience to get our attention or speak to us.

Words from God give life to the spirit, because they are Spirit and they are life (John 6:63). His words also bring freedom, for where the Spirit of the Lord is, there is freedom (2 Corinthians 3:17). His words release faith and cause us to put our trust in Him. God speaks the truth in love. He brings conviction, not condemnation. His word can bring a Godly rebuke because He disciplines those He loves (Hebrews 12:5-6).

Thoughts from God are usually encouraging and bear witness to His character and nature. They are opposite to our ways of thinking. *'For My thoughts are not your thoughts, neither are your ways My ways'* (Isaiah 55:8). His words are usually backed by scripture, though not always. However, they don't contradict scripture.

A word or thought from God brings revelation and clarity, instead of confusion. His word releases unity amongst Spirit-filled believers. There is no shame or failure in the Kingdom. God forgives when we truly repent. There is a sense of peace when we are in His will, or a word is from Him. He can always confirm His word to us in other ways when we ask. Sometimes, there can be a sense of urgency in His word, but it is usually a wake-up call to position and prepare His people. We can always ask God to confirm if a word or thought is from Him, and He will gladly do so.

During my time in Mozambique the question was popped in my mind if I would serve God in South Sudan. Immediately fear entered my heart as I thought I would be shot and not come back alive. This lie was from the enemy and attached to fear to stop me going. However, when I asked the Lord if it was His will, the fear lifted from my heart as quick as it came and His peace rested within me. Instantly, I knew it was His will and I followed Him.

Specific Discernment

Sometimes, specific discernment is required to see more clearly into things, especially when ministering to others. Some may have the gift to discern or distinguish between spirits, and this is known as the 'gift of discernment of spirits' (1 Corinthians 12:10). It is one of the revelatory gifts along with the gifts of wisdom and knowledge.

Some may have the ability to discern when angels are present. This may be through sight or spiritual awareness, where they can see or sense the angelic presence. These may be ministering angels of joy, healing, deliverance, breakthrough, prophecy or other warring angels.

Some may discern the function of demonic spirits that have influence over an individual, or church, or nation. This is useful when seeking God's strategy, be it for an individual, church or over a geographical area.

Spiritual discernment is an important asset for healing and deliverance ministry. For example, a person may be struggling with a problem but also have an underlying spirit that is to be discerned in order for the person to be set free and healed. Sometimes it may appear obvious by the ungodly fruit that is manifesting in a person's life, but other times it isn't. This is when we ask the Holy Spirit to reveal the underlying spiritual root. Many times when people have asked me to pray for a specific problem, the Lord has revealed an underlying spiritual root or cause to their problem.

Most times we are not aware of what we may be carrying until someone discerns through the Holy Spirit and brings it to light. The Lord will shine His light on a situation if we ask Him to reveal what spirit is operating behind a problem. Seers are usually good at discerning for they can see in the Spirit what is taking place in a given situation.

True versus False Discernment

It is important whenever we think we are 'discerning' something that we are not holding onto judgment. If we are, then we may be discerning with our flesh and not through the Spirit. Ungodly judgement creates false discernment. We are to be spiritually immune to judging others in order to spiritually discern what God is saying. We are to remove the plank from our own eye before we try to remove the speck from our brother's eye (Luke 6:41).

Francis Frangipane said we will never possess true discernment until we crucify our instincts to judge[1]. True discernment is rooted in love, whereas false discernment is rooted in criticism. False discernment is slow to hear, quick to speak and quick to anger. It carries judgment, condemnation, disunity, fear, control, gossip and rejection. On the other hand, true discernment is quick to hear, slow to speak and comes with restoration, redemption, reconciliation and peace.

Paul prayed for the Philippians that *their love* may abound more in the knowledge and depth of insight so that they may be able to *discern* what is best (Philippians 1:9). Love releases true discernment. However, let's not forget we must be shrewd as snakes and as innocent as doves (Matthew 10:16).

Sometimes, people may give advice and say it is from God when their underlying spirit is fear or control. They may call it wisdom, but true Wisdom is spoken in love and peace with no fear or other ungodly attachments, like control. False wisdom is rooted in fear, lies and insecurity. James says the Wisdom that comes from God is first pure, then peace loving, considerate, submissive, full of mercy and good fruit, impartial and sincere (James 3: 14-17).

We can't afford to continue to be tricked by the devil through deception and lack of discernment. The more we get to know someone, the more we will discern their ways and thoughts. Spiritual discernment is a necessary tool for our spiritual growth. As we listen to God and grow in our relationship with Him, we will come to discern His ways and recognise the moves of His Spirit.

ENDNOTES:

[1] Frangipane, Francis; *The Three Battlegrounds (Arrow Publications, 2006) p73.*

4

Power In the Blood

The blood of Jesus, His Son, purifies us from all sin

1 John 1:7

The blood of Jesus plays a crucial part in our healing and freedom. It has the power to heal, cleanse, forgive, break covenants and curses, deliver from sins and ungodly spirits, as well as the power to provide divine covering and protection. The enemy shrieks at the blood of Jesus because it is like some powerful, supernatural bleach that cleanses us from all filth and spiritual germs. No evil spirit can penetrate the blood of Jesus.

Mahesh Chavda, a healing evangelist, discovered the power of the blood of Jesus during a crusade many years ago in Africa. One night, he happened to be alone without a ministry team when thousands of people, especially witchdoctors and satanists, came to his crusade. He cried out to God and the Lord spoke these words to him in an audible voice, *'You are not alone, for I am your helper. Tonight I will give you a revelation of My blood!'*[1] There were apparently 800 sorcerers casting curses, and the African pastors were all afraid. Mahesh boldly declared these words on the stage: *'Tonight, God has shown me that one drop of the blood of Jesus can destroy the kingdom of Satan!'*[1] That night, the witchdoctors, sorcerers and satanists were delivered en masse without a single hand touching them. God's power was displayed through one drop of the blood of Jesus, as Mahesh boldly declared God's word to the people. The power of the blood of Jesus was demonstrated as Mahesh was supernaturally protected from the demons, and the satanists were radically delivered and healed. Then, the ex-satanists responded to the call, as they gave their lives to Jesus. A nation was changed in a day (Zechariah 3:9, Isaiah 66: 8).

Blood of the New Covenant

Partaking in the Communion, the body and blood of Jesus, plays a significant part in our lives and in the healing ministry. The Lord revealed this when I first took a medical team on an outreach in the bushes of Mozambique. One of the important parts of team preparation and unity was taking the Communion. This was an opportunity for the members of the team to humble themselves before God, get their hearts right and come under the covering of His blood. There was such a strong sense of unity in the Spirit amongst the team and divine covering every time this was done. This was essential before we stepped into the villages that were infiltrated with witchdoctors, shamanists and sorcerers.

On other occasions, the Holy Spirit may prompt me to offer Communion to individuals or couples, at the end of a ministry session. People can be set free from demonic covenants as they enter into a new covenant with Jesus, because His blood *is* the blood of the new covenant. I have seen relationships restored, people healed, and bondages broken, when Communion has been taken. Comm-union is coming-into-union with Jesus.

After ministering to a couple who were struggling in their marriage, I felt prompted to offer them Communion. As they both entered into Communion with the Lord, something happened in the Spirit that caused joy and reconciliation in their hearts. They both laughed in the Spirit as their hearts became reunited.

People who have been involved in the occult (including witchcraft, new age, martial arts, and freemasonry) may have knowingly or unknowingly, entered into ungodly covenants with evil spirits, especially the covenant with death. This is because oaths, vows or covenants are made to demonic spirits in such practices or secret societies.

Covenants made to ungodly spirits may be passed down the bloodline as a result of the sins of the parents and forefathers. Those who make covenants with demonic spirits, including those who have been dedicated to ancestral spirits, enter into a covenant with death. The Lord said: *'You boast "We have entered into a covenant with death, with the grave we have made an agreement...we have made a lie our refuge and falsehood our hiding place." So this is what the Sovereign Lord says: "See, I lay a stone in Zion, a tested stone, a precious cornerstone for a sure foundation; the one who trusts will never be dismayed...**Your covenant with death will be annulled; your agreement with the grave will not stand**,"'* (Isaiah 28:14-18).

In 2017, I was invited to minister at a church in Mozambique and during the worship the Lord highlighted the above passage from Isaiah 28:14-18. I was surprised for it was the passage that referred to the people who entered into a covenant with death. On discussing this with the pastor, he said it was customary for the people to be dedicated to the ancestral spirits when young, and as a result they would have entered in a covenant with death. The same thing had happened to him when he was very young. So we decided to do a session one afternoon on ancestral (generational) sins and curses. We discussed the list of ancestral sins that applied to his culture, including dedication to ancestral spirits, and it seemed right for the pastor to lead his people through this time of prayer ministry. After the hour long prayers for cleansing the blood-line it seemed appropriate for everyone to take Communion, and the pastor agreed to offer this to the people. Their covenants with death were annulled as they rededicated themselves to Jesus, and entered into a new covenant with Him. One young boy testified to experiencing the wind of the Holy Spirit enter him for the first time as he took the Communion. The Lord had set this boy free from the spirit of death and he was now connected to the Spirit of Life. Many other testimonies were given as people were set free and physically healed from the effects of ancestral sins and curses.

I met a Sudanese man who was aware his parents had dedicated him at some witchcraft ceremony when he was very young. He forgave his relatives for what they had done and repented of any oath or covenant that was made between him and satan. We broke any covenants made with death, through the power of the blood of Jesus. He then dedicated his life to Jesus, inviting Him to be his Lord and Saviour. Through the power of the blood of Jesus we can annul all ungodly covenants.

Zechariah prophesied: *'As for you, because of **the blood of My covenant with you, I will free your prisoners from the waterless pit**,'* (Zechariah 9:11). There is power in the blood as we enter in a new covenant with Jesus. It is through the blood of Jesus that we are cleansed, purified, healed, restored and redeemed. John said that the blood of Jesus purifies us from all sin (1 John 1:5-7). This implies we receive ongoing cleansing with the blood. Peter said we have been redeemed with the precious blood of Jesus and *'by His wounds (or stripes) you have been healed'* (1 Peter 1:18-19, 2:24).

The life of a creature is in the blood. Hence, God made the atonement of sin possible in the Old Testament through the sacrifice of an animal on the altar. However, the blood of Jesus now provides atonement for our sins. There is life in the blood and it is through the blood of Jesus that our sins can be forgiven (Hebrews 2:17).

Isaiah 53:4-5 says: *'Surely He took up our **infirmities** and carried our **sorrows**, yet we considered Him stricken by God, smitten by Him and afflicted. But He was pierced for our **transgressions**, He was crushed for our **iniquities;** the punishment that brought us peace was upon Him and **by His wounds we are healed**'.* This scripture is also referred to in Matthew 8:16-17: *'Many who were demon-possessed were brought to Him and He drove out the spirits with a word and healed all the sick. This was to fulfill what was spoken through the prophet Isaiah: "He took up our infirmities and carried our diseases"'.* The blood of Jesus not only forgives our sins, including our generational sins (or iniquities), but heals and sets us free, physically, emotionally and spiritually.

Sanctifying Power

One day whilst out walking, I was meditating on the power of the blood. It came to mind to ask God to show me what it would feel like to have a drop of His blood fall on me. I asked in faith believing He would reveal something, and next minute I experienced something quite extraordinary. From my head going down to my feet I felt a supernatural cleansing and purification like I had never felt before. It felt like some powerful supernatural bleach had just washed through my entire being. I felt whiter than the whitest of colours and purer than the purest of things. It was truly amazing. I felt like I was a transparent, spotless bride. His blood is like supernatural bleach that kills all known germs (or delivers from sickness and demons) and removes all stains (or sin) leaving a radiant, translucent white, bright colour without spot or blemish. His blood will sanctify us from all that is not of Him. There is power when we ask for the cleansing of His blood on our bodies where it has been contaminated by sickness, unclean spirits and sin.

Sanctified Imagination

One of the helpful tools for inner healing is a sanctified imagination. This can be compared to a cleansing or anti-septic solution that is applied to the body before an operation. Likewise, once the soul (mind, will, emotions and imagination) is cleansed through the sanctifying blood of Jesus, things may be more clearly seen in the Spirit during a healing session. When the imagination is cleansed and sanctified, this enables us to see and think in the supernatural as we engage our hearts with God (2 Corinthians 10:5).

How do we sanctify our minds, imagination and spirit? It may be done through surrendering our body, soul and spirit to Jesus, and coming under the influence of His Spirit (1 Thessalonians 5:23). As we do, we can ask Him to cleanse or sanctify our eyes, ears, feelings and imagination with His blood, so we may see, hear, feel and discern through the power of His Spirit. Likewise, we can take authority over any negative thoughts or distracting spirits, and ask Him to guard the entrances and exits to our hearts and minds, so we filter what we allow in and out (Ezekiel 44:5-6). Once we have cleansed our senses with His blood, we may invite His Spirit to lead us through the healing session, trusting He knows what needs to be done, as we engage our heart with His Spirit by faith (Ephesians 3:17).

Celebration of Passover

Jesus had eagerly desired to eat the Passover meal with His disciples. This was His last supper with them before he faced the cross. Today, we celebrate it as Holy Communion or the Eucharist.

The Passover was celebrated in remembrance of the night when the Israelites fled Egypt. This was the night when the plague of death and destruction 'passed over' the doorposts that were marked with the blood of a lamb. The Lord said: *'The blood will be a sign for you on the houses where you are; and when I see the blood, I will pass over you. No destructive plague will touch you when I strike Egypt,'* (Exodus 12:13). There was divine protection from the plague of death on the homes that were marked by the blood of a lamb.

When King Hezekiah celebrated the Passover feast with his people, he said this prayer:' *"May the Lord, who is good, pardon everyone who sets his heart on seeking God- the Lord, the God of his fathers- even if he is not clean according to the rules of the sanctuary." And the Lord heard Hezekiah **and healed** the people,'* (2 Chronicles 30:19-20). The Lord not only heard Hezekiah, but He *healed* the people. The Hebrew word used for 'healed' is *'Rapha'* [2] - the same word as in *Jehovah Rapha*, the Lord who heals. Hence, there was physical healing when they participated in the Passover meal.

The celebration of Passover in 2020 occurred during the peak of the Corona virus pandemic. I believe this was a significant timing and an opportunity to come under divine protection and receive divine healing through the power of Jesus' blood, as the 'plague' swept over the nations.

Power in the Communion

Many celebrate the Communion in remembrance of what Jesus did but don't necessarily believe it is the body and blood of Jesus. Instead, they see it as symbolic. However, there are other Christians who believe they are receiving the body and blood of Jesus. They believe something happens to it in the supernatural realm, whether before or after taking it. I believe that the Communion is a mystery and that something supernatural does take place after taking it. Otherwise Jesus would have said this is 'symbolic' or 'representative' of My body and blood. But He didn't. He said: *'This is My body'* and *'This is My blood'*. In Luke's Gospel of the last supper we read that Jesus took bread, broke it and gave it to His disciples saying: *"**This is My body** given to you; do this in remembrance of Me". After the supper He took the cup saying, "This **cup is the new covenant in My blood** which is poured out for you"* (Luke 22:19-21). Here, He is declaring a new covenant replacing the old one, which was the law given by Moses. As we take Communion we are saying yes to our commitment to Jesus. It is as if we are setting ourselves apart for Him until He returns for His bride.

Jesus said that He is the bread of life and that His body and blood are both real. There is life in the blood of Jesus. *'Whoever eats My flesh and drinks My blood **abides** in Me and I in him'* (John 6:56, NKJV). It was only when Jesus broke bread with the two disciples whom He spoke with on the road to Emmaus, that their eyes were opened and they saw it was the risen Lord (Luke 24:30-31).

Jesus told the Jews and His followers that whoever eats His flesh and drinks His blood abides in Him, and He in them. Many of His followers left Him when hearing this. He said: *'I tell you the truth, unless you eat the flesh of the Son of Man and drink His blood, you have no life in you. Whoever eats My flesh and drinks My blood has eternal life and I will raise him up at the last day. For **My flesh is real food and My blood is real drink. Whoever eats My flesh and drinks My blood remains in Me and I in him. This is the bread that came down from heaven**'* (John 6:53-59).

I don't believe we are to take Communion out of a sense of religious duty, but rather an attitude of coming before the feet of Jesus and surrendering our very selves to Him (1 Corinthians 11:23-32). This means coming before Him with repentance in our hearts as we repent of our sins, and then asking Jesus to cleanse our body, soul and spirit with His precious blood. Each time we partake in the Communion, we are 'communing' or coming back into union with the Lord Himself. Benny Hinn, a healing evangelist, encountered the Lord when he shared in the Communion with a group of charismatic Catholic nuns. He testified to experiencing the tangible Presence of the Lord, as if he was kneeling at the feet of Jesus. This was because he was communing with the Lord in the Communion.³

Many have experienced healing and freedom when taking Communion in a worthy manner. Some have been set free from ungodly covenants as they have entered a new covenant with Jesus. Others have been healed of cancer. A man testified to being healed of prostate cancer by simply choosing to take Communion each day and live by faith. Three months after making this decision, he was healed and no longer had the cancer.

Many times the Lord has prompted my spirit to take Communion, whether on my own or with others, and especially during seasons of fasting. We mustn't underestimate the power in taking Communion. It is more than eating bread and drinking juice or wine. As we take it by faith, I believe it mysteriously becomes His body and blood. Otherwise, things wouldn't happen if it was just juice and bread.

A baby is yoked to its mother via the umbilical cord so the toxic waste products produced by the baby's body can be exchanged for the good healthy nutritional substances delivered through the mother's blood. In the same way that a baby is yoked via the umbilical cord to its mother, so we are to be yoked to Jesus through His blood. His blood removes our toxic wastes or sins in exchange for His healthy nutritional substances that we receive from His Spirit, that is, His Kingdom DNA. We may be continually yoked to Him through abiding in His Presence and by daily cleansing ourselves with His blood.

Power in the Blood of Jesus

Here are some reminders of the power that's in the blood of Jesus.

His Blood Cleanses and Sanctifies Us from All Sin
His blood is like some supernatural bleach that purifies us from all our confessed sins (1 John 1:7). It cleanses our conscience from acts that lead to death, so that we may serve the living God! (Hebrews 9:14). In the Old Testament it was the blood of animals that made atonement for man's sins (Leviticus 17:11). How much more does the blood of Jesus make atonement for our sins? John said: '*He is the* **atoning sacrifice for our sins,** *and not only for ours*

but also for the sins of the world' (1 John 2:2). This doesn't give us an excuse to carry on sinning, but rather to keep our hearts right with God.

Thank You Jesus, for the power of Your blood to cleanse and sanctify the body, soul and spirit.

Purchased by God & Redeemed

'Do you not know that your body is a temple of the Holy Spirit, who is in you, whom you have received from God? You are not your own; you were bought at a price. Therefore, honour God with your body' (1 Corinthians 6:19-20). Jesus has redeemed us from our sin by paying the price through the shedding of His blood (Romans 3:23-25). It is through His sacrificial blood that we are brought back into relationship with God and made one again with Him.

The twenty-four elders who were standing before the Lamb at the throne of God sang: **'You were slain, and with Your blood You purchased men for God from every tribe and language and people and nation'** (Revelation 5:9). If we were purchased with the blood of Jesus, then our lives belong to God; they are no longer our own. God reminds me that I belong to Him and my life is no longer my own but His. That is His desire for all of us. We are to belong to Him and no-one else in this world, for man didn't purchase us, but God did.

Thank You Jesus, for the price You paid for me through the cross, so I can belong to You.

Our Royal Inheritance

Through His blood we are adopted into His royal family. If we have been adopted, this means we come under His royal bloodline. Those who are led by the Spirit of God have been adopted as children of God. If we have been adopted in God's family, then we are heirs with Christ (Romans 8:14-17). **'You have made them to be a kingdom and priests** *to serve our God, and they will reign on the earth'* (Revelation 5:9 10). We have been called to be His kings and priests through the purchase of His royal blood. The more we come to know the ways of God, the more we will understand our royal identity in Him.

Thank You Jesus, that Your blood has made it possible for me to be adopted and become a royal son or daughter, a prince or princess in Your Kingdom. Help me to grow and mature in my royal identity.

Access into the Presence of God (into the Holy of Holies)
As Jesus gave His last breath on the cross, the curtain of the temple was torn in two (Luke 23:45). This represented the curtain that separated the Holy place from the Most Holy place (or Holy of Holies) in the temple. It was now no more. Jesus made it possible for us to have direct access to the Father by His death on the cross (Hebrews 9:1-28). Therefore, we do not need to wait for the Day of Atonement for the high priest to enter the Holy of Holies or to access His Presence through a priest. Instead, we have access into the Presence of God through reverently entering through the veil, the torn flesh of Jesus (Hebrews 10:19-20).

Thank You Jesus, that You made the way for me to come to the Father and engage in His Presence, through Your sacrifice on the cross.

Heals all Sickness and Infirmities
Isaiah 53 foretold about Jesus and how He carried our infirmities and sorrows. Our infirmities refer to our sicknesses, and our sorrows refer to our emotional pain. He was pierced for our transgressions and crushed for our iniquities. Transgression refers to personal sin and iniquities refer to the sins passed down the bloodline, known as generational sin. '*And by **His wounds we are healed**' (Isaiah* 53:4-5). Our body, soul and spirit can receive healing through the power of His blood. It is not something that is automatically done, but it is available if we ask Jesus for it.

In the Old Testament, Isaiah prophesied that by His wounds *we are healed*. This was prophesied in the present tense and in the New Testament, Peter said: *'He Himself bore our sins in His body on the tree so that we might die to sins and live for righteousness; by **His wounds you have been healed**'* (1 Peter 2:24). By faith we are to claim this truth as we step into our healing through the power of His blood. There is atonement in the blood of Jesus.

Thank You Jesus, that the power of Your blood can bring healing to our body, soul and spirit. I receive this by faith with thanksgiving.

Delivers from the Enemy
The prophet Zechariah declared, '*As for you, because of the blood of My covenant with you, I will free your prisoners from the waterless pit*' (Zechariah 9:11). His blood not only heals us, but it delivers us from the enemy's camp. We overcome by the blood of the Lamb (Revelation 12:11).

Thank You Jesus, that Your blood of the new covenant deliverers me from the hands of the enemy.

Protection by the Blood
The Israelites were protected from death and destruction by marking their doorposts with the blood of a lamb. The enemy cannot penetrate the blood of Jesus, hence we can pray for protection and covering by the blood, from any demonic power or sickness.

Whether I'm doing ministry, or travelling, or simply at home, I regularly pray for the blood of Jesus to cover and protect me. It is like a supernatural covering that prevents the enemy from knowing my plans or coming my way. In the same way we spray our plants to be protected from bugs, or put out pellets to keep away the slugs, so we can cover ourselves with the blood of Jesus to be protected from the enemy.

On one occasion I asked a friend to join me in praying for a woman whom I felt needed to be delivered from a spirit of infirmity that was behind her sickness. I quickly, but silently, put the blood of Jesus between me and the sick person but my friend did not. After the woman got set free and healed, I was fine but my friend felt an oppressive spirit come on her, because she hadn't covered herself with the blood of Jesus. She was fine again after prayer, but this proved the importance of protecting ourselves with His blood when we are ministering to people or entering enemy territory or advancing the Kingdom.

Thank You Jesus, that Your blood has power to cover and protect us from demonic spirits, infections and hide us from the enemy.

Breaks Curses
Jesus took all curses on the cross by becoming a curse for us. '*Christ redeemed us from the curse of the law by becoming a curse for us,*

for it is written: "Cursed is everyone who is hung on a tree!"' (Galatians 3:13). Hence we can break the power of a curse spoken over us or someone else through the power of the blood of Jesus. It is as simple and as powerful as that.

Thank You Jesus, that I can break all curses through the power of Your blood.

Redeems from the Sins of Our Forefathers
Peter says we were redeemed from the sins of our forefathers with the precious blood of Christ. *'For you know that it was not with perishable things like silver or gold that* **you were redeemed from the empty ways of life handed down to you by your forefathers, but with the precious blood of Christ, a lamb without blemish or defect'** (1 Peter 1:18-19). The blood of Jesus can break off any curse and cleanse us from all generational sin. We do not have to live under the sins and curses of our forefathers but can be set free through His blood.

Thank You Jesus, that Your blood has power to forgive and cleanse me from every generational sin and curse.

Unity in the Spirit through the Blood
Jesus told His disciples to take Communion on a regular basis until He returns. As we come together as fellow believers and participate in His Communion, I believe there is a unity in the Spirit. When people gather together to take Communion and repent of their sin and forgive one another, then unity is restored amongst the group of believers. Communion can be a powerful way to restore unity where there has been division in the body.

Thank You Jesus, for the power of Your blood to restore unity where there has been division in the body of Christ.

Victory in the Blood
We overcome by the blood of the lamb (Revelation 12:11). There is victory in the blood. Jesus defeated Satan at the cross: *'And having disarmed the powers and authorities, He made a public spectacle of them, triumphing over them by the cross'* (Colossians 2:15). We have authority from God to overcome all power of the enemy, even death itself, through the power of Jesus' blood! Death has lost its

sting for it has been swallowed up in the victory. Jesus overcame all death through His sacrificial death on the cross for us.

During an outreach in Mozambique, it was interesting to see the reaction of a woman of another faith when she noted a red cross on our medical tent. It turned out that she was a witchdoctor and her comment was one of fear as she saw the red cross and shrieked 'that's the blood of Jesus!' It made me realize how Satan and his evil hordes fear the blood of Jesus for they know that it will overcome and conquer any demonic power or evil spirit. They cannot penetrate the blood of Jesus but instead shriek back in fear and dread, and run from it. Satanists, witchdoctors and sorcerers usually obtain their demonic power through the blood from animal or child 'sacrifices'. Jesus, who was without sin, sacrificed His own blood, which was pure and spotless, so we could be redeemed from the clutches of Satan and be brought back into a love relationship with God.

Thank You Jesus, for the power of Your blood to overcome death and all the works of the enemy.

There is power and victory with the blood of Jesus. It not only cleanses us from all sin and heals us of all sickness and infirmities, but it can unite, protect, and overcome all the works of the enemy. Let us not underestimate the power in the Communion and the blood.

END-NOTES

[1] Chavda, Mahesh; *The Hidden Power of the Blood of Jesus;* (2004, Destiny Image) p10
[2] Rapha (Hebrew 7495); *Strong's Expanded Exhaustive Concordance: Red Letter Edition*
[3] Hinn, Benny; *The Blood;* (Charisma House, 2006) p 192-193

HEALING TOOLS

5

Curses, Vows & Covenants

*Your covenant with death will be annulled,
your agreement with the grave will not stand*

Isaiah 28:18

Curses, vows and covenants can be made knowingly or unknowingly, and they can be passed down the bloodline affecting the present and future generations. Curses, vows and covenants affect everyone, whether they have been made by ourselves or others.

Curses

The Oxford English dictionary states a curse is: *'A solemn appeal to a supernatural power to inflict harm on someone or something'*. This may be to an individual, a group of people, a family, a house, a work place or business, a village or church or even a nation. So a curse may be inflicted on anyone or anything.

A curse may come through sin. When Cain killed Abel, God said that his sin had brought him under a curse (Genesis 4:11). God made it clear that when we obey His commands blessings are released, but if we disobey His commands, then curses are released (Deuteronomy 11:26). He goes on to list all the sins that will release curses, and then lists the blessings if people choose to obey Him (Deuteronomy 27-28). This isn't because God is harsh, but because sin opens the door for the enemy to inflict curses, whereas obedience opens the door for the Lord to bless. *'But if you do not do what is right, sin is crouching at your door; it desires to have you, but you must master it'* (Genesis 4:7).

Jesus took all our sins and *all* our curses on the cross. He became our curse through His one perfect sacrifice on the cross for us. *'Christ redeemed us from the law by becoming a curse for us, for it is written: "Cursed is everyone who is hung on a tree,"'* (Deuteronomy 21:23, Galatians 3:13). We no longer have to live under the power or effect of a curse, because by the power of the blood of Jesus we can be freed from all curses.

Proverbs tells us that death or life are in the power of the tongue and that reckless words pierce like a sword but the tongue of the wise brings healing (Proverbs 18:21, 12:18). James tells us not to be hypocrites who praise God one moment, then out of the same mouth *curse* our friends and neighbours (James 3:9-10). We all have the ability to curse, simply by saying negative words about ourselves or others! There is power in our tongue and the words we speak. Our words can bring blessings and life if they are from God, but curses or death if they are from the enemy. Without realizing, we may have cursed many including ourselves, or come under a curse by agreeing with the negative words spoken by others. If so, then we can repent and break the power of the words in the Name of Jesus. Since Jesus took all of our curses on the cross, we can ask Him to cleanse us with the sanctifying power of His blood.

One day I was challenged when I heard someone speak on fasting from *negativity.* It's amazing how many negative words or thoughts we think or say in just a day. When we fast from negative words, we become aware of how often we say words of judgment, criticism, or unbelief. Fasting from negative words is a great spiritual exercise to help us stop speaking negatively about ourselves or others. Instead of saying or thinking negative thoughts like, *'I am no good at this,'* or *'I'm blind as a bat,'* or *'I'm always...'*, *'You are hopeless, rubbish, will never do anything, you're always...'*, we can say divine truths like, *'I can do all things through Christ,'* and *'He who is in me is greater than him in the world,'* and *'With God all things are possible'* as we choose to bless ourselves and others by speaking positively.

It is good to reverse a curse with a blessing. We can ask God to bless those who curse us or whom we have cursed. Jesus said that we are not only to forgive our enemies but to *bless* our enemies and *those who curse us* (Mathew 5:44, Luke 6:28). Paul says not to repay evil with evil but overcome evil with good (Romans 12:12-21). A blessing is actually a weapon that quenches the effects of a curse. We bless others by praying God will touch them and for His love to come in their lives, instead of saying negative things that will invite the enemy to inflict evil or harm.

On one occasion I became ill within twenty-four hours of arriving in South Sudan. I felt weak and lethargic, with a low grade fever and persistent nausea. I thought I'd caught an infection on the plane. No medication seemed to help. So I asked a fellow missionary if she would pray for me. As she prayed, she felt led by the Spirit to break a curse over me in Jesus' Name. As soon as she did this, my spirit responded and my body started to feel better instantly. Praise God that we can break curses with the power of His Name and through the power of His blood. Curses are real and exist in everyday life and may even be behind sickness or other things.

Proverbs says how an undeserved curse doesn't come to rest (Proverb 26:2). In other words, as long as we don't come into agreement with the curse or open a door in our heart to the curse through fear or judgement, then the curse or negative word spoken, should not harm us. Jesus said we are not to judge if we don't want to be judged (Matthew 7:1).

On one occasion whilst in Mozambique, I went with a friend to get a cool, refreshing drink when I suddenly developed an intense band of pain around my head. The pain level was gradually increasing and it felt like someone was tightening a metal band with screws around my head. I had never experienced this head pain and instantly knew I was being cursed. I asked my friend to pray for me and as she did, she broke the curse in Jesus' name. The pain started to go, as quickly as it came.

Another lady came to me with a two month old baby. One day she was breastfeeding fine, then the next day she had no milk. It just stopped. She was a well-built lady and her breasts also well-developed. I examined her and, sure enough, no milk came out of either breast. I found her story hard to believe until the

Holy Spirit brought to my attention that this was a curse. I broke any curses off her breasts and spoke blessings over her and for milk to flow forth again. She tested one breast and out squirted milk. She looked excited then tested the other. Milk also came out. Tears welled up in her eyes. As simply as the curse came, it was just as easily broken in the powerful Name of Jesus and replaced with a blessing.

During another clinic, an old-looking lady presented with a history of weight loss, no appetite, no thirst and feeling very weak and lethargic. On examining her, there was nothing to find to suggest any serious illness including no signs of significant anaemia, enlarged organs or abnormal masses. Her examination was actually normal apart from her looking very lethargic and oppressed. I asked her if anything happened around the time she started to waste away. She said she had been to a 'ceremony' and openly admitted that she had been cursed by someone and then deteriorated after that. With no further explanation, she was willing to forgive her enemy and ask Jesus to forgive her. We broke off the spirit of death and any curses spoken over her and declared life and health in the Name of Jesus. Then we tested her body out. She was able to walk unaided for a fair distance. When she came back, she had no difficulty eating a sandwich and could drink water in a normal fashion. I told her she wasn't going to die but live, for the curses were broken and we had replaced them with a blessing.

Cursed Village
I was visiting a village in Mozambique with the medical team, when most of the people presented to the clinic with the same problem. There were children, young adults and older people, who presented with some degree of generalized body pain which affected mainly their limbs and joints. All of them had this pain for the past two months! It suddenly came to mind that these people could have had curses spoken over them around two months ago by someone that may have cursed the village. There was no medical explanation for all the different ages to have pain in their joints and back, with no other medical symptoms (such as fever, malaise, sore throat, rash, diarrhoea, etc.), especially since they all seemed relatively well on examination. I suddenly

informed my colleague of what the Lord had shown me and we broke off the curses over each person in Jesus' Name and blessed their bodies with His health and peace. Everyone we prayed for was instantly healed. On that occasion I ended up giving out very little, if any medicines, for they simply got better once the curse was broken.

How to Break a Curse

Curses can be broken directly when they have been inflicted by another person. However, if a curse has been self-inflicted, then we can repent of speaking any negative words before breaking the curse. Once we recognize the negative word-curses we have spoken, whether against ourselves or others, we can ask God for forgiveness.

A curse can be broken in the powerful Name of Jesus, or with the powerful blood of Jesus. Sometimes we don't know who said the curse but may discern there is a curse behind a problem or symptom. If that is the case then simply break it: *'I break the curse in the Name of Jesus'* or *'I break every curse by the blood of Jesus'*. We can thank Jesus for taking all our curses on the cross.

Jesus told us to bless those who curse us. This is because a blessing carries power and quenches enemy activity. It is like pouring burning coals on the enemy's head (Romans 12:20). We can choose to go in the opposite spirit by loving our enemy and praying for them to know God's love and healing power in their hearts. And as we bless and pray for our enemies, it may release further healing to our bodies.

Vows

A vow is an oath or promise. Some may say, 'I swear by...' or 'I vow...' or 'I promise...' or 'I will never...' or 'I will always...' Most ungodly vows are usually made in haste, whereas Godly vows such as a wedding vow or a vow to God, are given more time and thought. Ungodly vows are usually made when we are feeling angry, upset or thinking negatively about ourselves or others. It is easy to make ungodly vows after a painful experience or outburst of anger. How many times have we said in a tone of anger, disappointment or hurt, 'I will never...', 'I will always...' 'I promise I will...'? These are ungodly vows that lead to bondage. Sometimes, we may make friendship vows that can no longer be kept. These too may need to be broken.

Vows are treated in the same way as curses. Don't forget we may need to forgive others for what they said or did, or forgive ourselves for making the vow.

An African elderly man asked for prayer for his lower abdominal pain. He had it for some years and believed it was renal. He had been to the hospital and nothing that the doctors gave him worked. The tests showed nothing. I asked him what happened around the time this pain came. He said he fell out with his father. His father wanted to give his cows to another son so the man got jealous and started to curse his father. His father cursed him back in return. This man vowed to never speak to his father again. After discussion, he agreed to forgive his father and repent for his own sins and feelings of anger, hatred, and unforgiveness. He broke the vows and curses he said and then asked Jesus to heal him. When I laid hands on him, he started to cry. He was shaking and profusely sweating. At the end, he smiled and wiped his face. The pain had left him and he was now at peace being set free from bondage.

A friend had made a vow with her identical twin sister when they were young. They made a vow that they would be the closest of friends forever. It seemed beautiful and sweet until one of the sisters got married and everything changed. The other sister started to experience deep grief when she realized she was no longer her sister's best friend. I explained the vow had become an unhealthy soul-tie which needed to be broken. She agreed and surrendered the relationship to God. She repented of the vow and broke the power of the words in Jesus' name. After this she felt a peace and joy, as the grief lifted. She still loved her sister, but was no longer yoked by the vow. Instead, she became free to get married herself.

Vows are powerful and may block healing unless addressed, especially the vow to never forgive, or never tell anyone. The Holy Spirit is quick to reveal hidden vows or negative words, in order to heal our body, soul and spirit, and restore our relationship with God.

How to Break a Vow
Vows are dealt with the same way as curses. First we are to recognize we have made an ungodly vow. Usually, the Holy Spirit reminds us what vow was made and when. We can give this to God along with any anger, pride, hurt or whatever emotion was expressed at the time the vow was made. Then we break the vow and declare it powerless in Jesus' Name!

Covenants

A covenant is an oath made between two people, or between a person and God or a person and demonic spirit, and is stronger than a vow. It has usually been given considerable thought and is legally or spiritually binding[1]. Covenants can be verbal or written. The most common covenants we know are marriage covenants. On the wedding day a couple will take vows followed by signing a legal document. They are entering into a covenantal relationship, choosing to be faithful to this person until he or she dies.

In some parts of the world, the strongest type of covenant made between two friends is known as a blood covenant. This covenant is made when the blood of two people is intermingled. This is not entered into lightly for a blood covenant is kept until death. The most common type is where the palms or wrists of both individuals are cut with a knife to create a flow of blood. Then the hands are shaken or the wrists are held tightly together. This is not just a verbal agreement, but a spiritual bonding takes place to be faithful to the other until death. Some believe this is what happened in the relationship between David and Jonathan, as they became 'one in spirit'. *'Jonathan became one in spirit with David, and he loved him as himself,'* (1 Samuel 18:1).

Some may knowingly or unknowingly make covenants with the devil or demonic spirits. For example, this may occur when young children or babies are traditionally dedicated to their ancestral spirits. However, others may use the blood of animals or human blood in exchange for demonic power, and use this power for inflicting curses, sicknesses, death, witchcraft, or for gaining control over others. Any pact made with demonic spirits is to be repented of and renounced, and broken through the sanctifying blood of Jesus.

A lady asked for prayer concerning the curses and demonic covenants made by her grandfather, who was a high ranking freemason. She sensed she was under the influence of the oaths and covenants made by her grandfather, and wanted to be healed and set free. After she forgave her grandfather and renounced the various oaths, she struggled to break free from the covenant with death. As we interceded, she finally broke the covenant, and I had a strong sense she was to take the Communion. She was to enter into a new covenant with Jesus by partaking in His body and blood. Jesus said: *'This is My blood of the new covenant which is poured out for many for the forgiveness of sins,'* (Matthew 26:28). As she did, she crossed over from a covenant with death into a new covenant with Jesus. Jesus is the Resurrection and the Life (John 11:12). The Communion played a powerful part in the process of setting her free. This wasn't planned but rather prompted by the Holy Spirit.

Isaiah referred to the people who made a covenant with death: *'You boast, "We have entered into a **covenant with death**, with the grave we have made an agreement. When an overwhelming scourge sweeps by, it can't touch us, for we have made a lie our refuge and falsehood our hiding place." So this is what the Sovereign Lord says: "See, I lay a stone in Zion, a tested stone, a precious cornerstone for a sure foundation; the one who trusts will never be dismayed...Your **covenant with death will be annulled;** your agreement with the grave will not stand.."'* (Isaiah 28:14-18). Hence, Jesus our cornerstone, who was tested on the cross, has the power and authority to annul all ungodly covenants.

When covenants are made to demonic spirits a person enters in a covenant with death. The American apostle, Robert Henderson, expands further by saying: '***People in our ancestry made covenants with demonic spirits to protect, provide for, prosper, and empower them.*** *This is true in every culture and in every race of people....**These covenants created by trading in the spirit realm are active until someone annuls them... Somewhere in their bloodline demonic powers have been given the right to own them. These rights have to be revoked. When they are, the demon forces lose the right to hold people in sickness.*'[1] (Bold print mine).

The covenants made to the spirit realm are legally binding until they are annulled. They may be the cause of sickness, disease, poverty and even death. Ungodly trade deals may have been made through agreements in business deals, or coming under ungodly leadership, or any trading which was in effect partnering with an ungodly spirit. These legally binding trade deals may affect future generations until they have been repented of, forgiven and annulled. Ungodly covenants are annulled by the power of the blood of Jesus, for we are forgiven by His blood (Isaiah 28:18).

In the book of Ezekiel, the Lord made a covenant with the New Jerusalem, the bride of Christ: *'Later I passed, and when I looked at you and saw that you were old enough for love, I spread the corner of my garment over you and covered your nakedness. I gave you **my solemn oath and entered into a covenant with you,** declares the sovereign Lord, **and you became mine,'*** (Ezekiel 16:8). This passage refers to the spiritual growth and maturity of the bride of Christ, such that, as we reach a particular stage in our relationship with Jesus, He will invite us into a covenantal relationship with Him.

In the Old Testament, a covenant was made between God and man through the blood taken from animal sacrifices. After sprinkling the blood of calves on the scrolls and people, Moses said: *'This is the blood of the covenant which God has commanded you to keep,'* (Hebrews 9:19-20). This first blood covenant was between God and His chosen people.

However, Jesus came to make a new and better blood covenant between God and man. This was an invitation for us to enter into a blood covenantal relationship with Jesus. Jesus invited you and me to enter into a covenantal relationship with Him, when He said, *'This is My blood of the New Covenant, which is poured out for you,'* (Luke 22:20). He was making a blood covenant with us, that is, the deepest form of relationship between two friends. Since friendships are two-way, then this means we are to engage in this covenantal relationship with Him, in order for it to be valid. However, sin breaks our covenant with Jesus, but each time we partake in the Communion and receive His forgiveness for our sins, we are renewing our covenant with Him. Jesus said the greatest love we can have is to lay down our life for our friends

(John 15:13). Just as Jesus demonstrated His sacrificial love for us on the cross, so He is inviting us to lay down our lives for Him.

So a blood covenant is the strongest binding covenant that is made unto death. Many have inherited legally binding covenants as a result of the covenants made by their ancestors. Hence, we can repent of any covenant we may have made or unknowingly inherited, especially legally binding covenants made through child sacrifice. Through the power of forgiveness and the sanctifying work of the blood of Jesus, we can declare these covenants annulled.

Curses, vows, and covenants, are like bolts on the doors of our hearts that prevent us from walking in freedom and keep us in bondage. All we have to do is ask the Holy Spirit to highlight any curses, vows or ungodly covenants we may have made or come under. As the Holy Spirit draws our attention to any, we can break them in the name of Jesus, or ask the Lord to annul them through the forgiving power of His blood. In doing so, we are unlocking the bolts on the doors of our hearts to receive healing and freedom.

ENDNOTES:

[1] Henderson, Robert; *Receiving Healing from the Courts of Heaven; (Destiny Image Publishers, 2018) p78*

6

Power of Forgiveness

Forgive your brother from your heart

Matthew 18:35

Forgiveness is a spiritual weapon. It is one of the most important tools, if not the most important, to release healing and freedom. Unforgiveness is like a bolt on the door of our hearts that keeps us in bondage, whereas forgiveness unbolts the door of our hearts and frees us from bondage. The power of forgiveness is often misunderstood and underestimated. Forgiveness is a choice and when we choose to release others or ourselves from past or present offenses, regrets and hurts, healing and freedom is released to our body, soul and spirit.

Why Should We Forgive?

There are three reasons why we are to forgive. The first reason is because forgiveness is a Kingdom principle. Jesus said if we want God to forgive us, then we are to forgive others: *'Do not judge and you will not be judged. Do not condemn, and you will not be condemned.* **Forgive, and you will be forgiven,**' (Luke 6:37). If we are willing to forgive, then Our Father will forgive us. Jesus taught us to pray: *'Forgive us for our sins, as we forgive those who sin against us'* (Matthew 6:12-14).

The second reason why we should forgive is because forgiveness powerfully releases healing and freedom to our body, soul and spirit. It has an effect on our physical, emotional and spiritual wellbeing. When we choose to forgive, we are the ones who are being set free from bondage. Many of our physical pains, heavy burdens, and chronic symptoms may be the result of harbouring unforgiveness in our hearts. I have witnessed so many people receive physical healing as a result of forgiving others, or themselves. A lady testified to pain leaving her hips after she forgave her father for abusing her, and she wasn't even praying for her hips to be healed.

The third reason to forgive is because forgiveness connects our hearts to others and to God, fulfilling the first two commandments, to love God and to love our neighbour.

How Do We Forgive?
Jesus said we are to forgive *from the heart*. He gave us the example of the servant who owed his master a huge sum of money. His master chose to forgive him and release him from his debt. However, another man happened to owe this servant some money, but the servant refused to forgive him. When the master heard about this, he made his servant pay back all he owed, because he refused to show mercy to this man. Jesus said: *'This is how My heavenly Father will treat each of you unless you* **forgive your brother from your heart'** (Matthew 18:21-35).

To forgive from our heart means we free the offender from owing us anything. There are no 'ifs' or 'buts'. One way of doing this is to imagine ourselves giving our offender a hand shake or a hug or inviting them for a drink (even when they don't deserve it) and releasing them from owing us anything. Sometimes it is not enough to just say, 'I forgive'. We have to really mean it and let go of all the things they have said or done that have offended or caused us pain. We can do this with God's amazing grace. If we ask Him for grace, He will give it to us, that is, the spiritual strength and ability to reach out to our enemies with His love.

When I hear people rattle aloud, 'Lord, I forgive Jo Bloggs for this...' and sense no emotion in their heart, I usually stop them in their tracks. Then I tell them to imagine the person they are to forgive is standing in front of them (even if they are dead). As they do, I ask them to look in to the person's eyes and speak directly to the person from their heart. Their tone of voice and words suddenly change. More words are spoken as they speak directly to the person, since it is coming from their heart. For example, they may say, 'Jo Bloggs, I forgive you for when you did this or said that to me. It hurt me...I no longer hold this against you...I let you off the hook....you owe me nothing. I pray the Lord will reveal His love to you and bless you.'

I met a lady with chronic hip pain who had received prayer but the pain remained. On questioning if she needed to forgive anyone, she said no and that she had forgiven all her enemies. I was somehow convinced she hadn't. This time I asked her if she had forgiven them from her heart and she admitted that she hadn't. After she decided to do this, the pain completely went from her hip.

You may argue that you can't possibly forgive a person for what they did to you, but Jesus did. He was betrayed by His own men, mocked, spat upon, slandered, physically beaten and tortured to the point His body was bruised, bleeding and disfigured. Jesus prayed these words on the cross: *'Father forgive them, for they know not what they are doing'* (Mathew 23:34). I believe with the same grace that Jesus had, we too can choose to forgive those who have badly hurt, abused, betrayed or mistreated us. We can simply ask Jesus for His grace to forgive. Grace is God's supernatural strength and ability to help us in our time of need. If we choose to forgive and be at peace with others, then we will keep ourselves free from any spirit of bondage or toxins linked to the unforgiveness. Forgiveness cleanses us from toxins and heals our bones (Proverbs 3:7-8).

One of the ways to forgive our worst enemies is for us to ask God how He sees the person who hurt us. When we see the person from God's perspective, there is then the grace to forgive. A friend struggled to forgive her work boss who continually intimidated her, until she asked God how He saw her boss. Suddenly, she had a picture of a little girl who was insecure and felt unloved. Instantly, she had the grace to forgive her boss when she saw her from God's heart.

A lady came to me with a painful, stiff shoulder. She had seen doctors and physiotherapists with little improvement. She had two levels of pain. One level had been ongoing and chronic since she fell on her shoulder when her son jumped on her back many years ago. This had caused reduced movement where she was unable to lift her arm above her head. The other level was more acute, and came after she heard disturbing information from her husband. So first, I asked her if she would forgive her husband. As she forgave him for what he had done with tears in her eyes, her acute pain left her shoulder. However, she still struggled to lift her shoulder above her head for it had been stiff since she had the accident with her son. I asked her to now forgive her son, but she adamantly said she had nothing against him and it was an accident. However, though she had a good relationship with her son, she probably felt angry and spoke negative words at the time of the accident. So she agreed to forgive him and repent of any anger or bitterness she had felt or expressed in the past to him. After doing this, she lifted up her arm in utter surprise and had full range of movement for the first time in years. She was astonished that the two levels of pain were both the result of unforgiveness from deep seated hurts towards her son and husband.

Unforgiveness is actually a sin and can keep us in spiritual, emotional and physical bondage. It is only when we choose to forgive the person who has hurt us *and release them of owing us anything*, that in turn we can be released and set free from the bondage it has put us in. This doesn't mean the offender isn't guilty, but rather that we are choosing not to judge them but hand the person over to God instead. James says there is only one Judge who is able to save and destroy (James 4:12). We are not to judge, but hand people over to God who is the Judge of all judges.

On a trip to Zambia, I met an old man who limped in with a walking stick. He had been limping for nearly forty years as the result of a negligent car crash by another man. He came for more analgesia and told me he was a Christian. I asked if he had forgiven the drunk driver who injured him. The answer was no. *Was he willing to?* Initially his facial expression said, 'Why should I?' After all, it was the drunk driver's fault. But I told him it's the kindness of God that leads to repentance (Romans 2:4). After explaining that God releases His healing power when we choose to forgive, he gave a deep sigh and decided to do it. He repented for his bitterness and unforgiving heart and chose to forgive the person who caused his disability. He then asked Jesus to heal and restore his leg. I took the stick from him and asked God to reverse what had happened to his leg in the Name of Jesus. After inviting him to get up, I held his hand and he got up to walk. At first he wobbled and then he walked straight. He not only walked, but he ran. He left the clinic physically healed, emotionally and spiritually set free with his walking stick held over his shoulders. Forgiveness brings physical healing as well as spiritual and emotional freedom.

A local lady came to an African church and specifically asked for prayer for her abdominal pain. She had been having stomach aches for two weeks with no diarrhoea or vomiting and no other accompanying gastro-intestinal symptoms. She had been to a witchdoctor at some point in her life. We first prayed against the witchcraft and spoke healing to her abdomen, but she felt no better. Then I thought there may be a curse on her, so we broke any curse. She felt worse after this. (The fact she was feeling worse with prayer made me think it was spiritually related.) Next, I asked if there was anyone she needed to forgive whom she didn't like or felt resentful towards. She nodded yes. It had been the same time when she fell out with this person that her symptoms started. She cried as she forgave the woman who hurt her by having an affair with her husband. After this, her abdomen was healed. She said she felt something leave her abdomen and there was no more pain. I believe there was a spirit of unforgiveness behind her abdominal pain and it left as soon as she dealt with it.

On another occasion, a staff member asked me for medicine for his wife who was at home with 'renal' pain. On further questioning, the pain seemed like chronic muscular and not necessarily renal in origin, though it appeared in the loin area. I got him to ask her if she needed to forgive anyone. Yes, her mother! So the husband went home and passed this information onto his wife. She prayed with her husband and forgave her mother from all the things she had said and ever done to her. Then her loin pain disappeared. I didn't see this woman or pray for her. She just responded to the advice, and after forgiving her mother she was instantly healed.

On a trip to Zimbabwe, I saw a man who had chronic lower back pain and right knee pain. He put it down to stressful labour from working in the mines. He had been partly healed of the pain after a session on forgiveness. So I asked if there was anyone he still needed to forgive. It turned out he hadn't forgiven his grandmother for cursing him as a child. After he decided to forgive her from his heart, his pain was completely gone. With a smile on his face, he demonstrated full range of movement with his knee and back. He asked if he should go and see her. I gave him the choice, and mentioned it could be an opportunity to witness God's love to her.

This is the power of forgiveness when we forgive from the heart. I have seen so many cases when people choose to forgive their enemies, where they experience spiritual freedom and physical and emotional healing. It is not about whether the perpetrator or offender deserves to be forgiven for God is the Judge who will make that decision. Instead, it is about setting ourselves free from bondage.

Toxic Poisons

Unforgiveness is usually connected to other negative emotions. These negative feelings are like toxins or poisons which can attack any part of our body. They include the feelings of *hatred (including self-hate), bitterness, jealousy, self-righteous anger, judgement, resentment, self-pity and revenge.* In extreme measures, unforgiveness may open the door in our heart for murderous or suicidal thoughts to enter. Many may say word-curses like 'I wish they were dead....I wish this happened to them....' or make ungodly vows like 'I will never forgive them or myself ...I will always hate them or myself...I will get my revenge...I will make sure they pay for this'.

In order to receive freedom and healing, we are to address these negative feelings, including word-curses and ungodly vows, and hand each one to Jesus. Negative feelings, like bitterness, anger, unforgiveness and so on, may come with a demonic spirit. It may start off as a negative emotion but the more we entertain it, we open our hearts to the spirit behind it. Hence, we may have to command the spirit of anger, spirit of bitterness, spirit of hatred, etc. to leave us in Jesus' Name. It is a lie to believe that we have a right to be angry when someone has done us wrong. This is self-righteous anger. In believing this lie, we open ourselves up to the spirit of hatred and bitterness as well as judgment and unforgiveness.

James said the tongue is a restless evil *full of deadly poison* (James 3:8). Bitter roots are like weeds which grow bigger if they are not up rooted or dealt with. They defile the body, soul and spirit with the evil poison they carry. We are to recognise bitter roots so we don't allow them to grow, but immediately uproot them. *'Make every effort to live in peace with all men and be holy...and see to it that no bitter root grows up to cause trouble and defile many,'* (Hebrews 12:14-15). Bitterness and negative words can defile the body of Christ and spread like a disease. Instead of agreeing with such words, we can choose to speak the truth in love and pray for those who offend us. I have seen people with swollen and even twisted joints who were full of bitterness and hatred to others or themselves, but the moment they forgave, their joints were healed. As we decide to let our offenders off the hook so they no longer owe us anything, we ourselves end up being set free and healed. I believe that's how it works.

There are many scriptures describing how our attitude affects our body. *'Fear the Lord and shun evil'* this will **'bring health to your body and nourishment to your bones'** (Proverbs 3:7-8). Also, *'A **heart at peace gives life to the body** but envy rots the bones'* (Proverbs 14:30). Likewise, *'A **cheerful heart is good medicine but a crushed spirit dries up the bones'*** (Proverbs 17:22). We can learn from these proverbs for there is profound truth and wisdom concerning how our emotions and spirit can affect our health and bones!

What Happened Around the Time the Person got Sick?

It is good to find out what happened in someone's life around the time they started to develop the symptoms or body pain. They may have had an unpleasant experience that led to feeling hurt or angry. Or it may be the person hates themselves for something they did. This may be the root to their body symptoms.

One lady I met in the UK had painful arthritic joints and asked me to pray for her. Before I did, I asked her if she had fallen out with anyone around the time she developed the pain or needed to forgive anyone who had offended her. She said no, and was then convicted by the Holy Spirit of her mother-in-law. It had all started after she fell out with her mother-in-law. After she repented of her negative feelings to her mother-in-law and forgave her mother-in-law of how she mistreated her, we then prayed for her joints to be healed. She sat on the floor, and for the first time in ages could get up with ease from the floor. Her joints were completely pain free. She commented that she hadn't been able to do that in a long time and had never thought the two were related.

What if the Pain Returns?
Unforgiveness may be the root cause to chronic body pain. I have seen people healed of pain in their shoulders, back, knees, hips, limbs, abdomen, neck and pelvis (basically anywhere in the body) when they have been willing to forgive others from their heart. However, symptoms may return after receiving healing but that doesn't mean the person wasn't healed originally. They are to be careful not to allow any similar seed or spiritual root to grow back again. Peter asked Jesus how many times are we to forgive, seven times? And Jesus replied seventy times seven, meaning forgiveness is something to do daily (Matthew 18:21).

I saw an old African lady who was of another faith and bent double, and came to me for pain relief. I prayed for her back and the Lord mercifully healed her immediately without her repenting of any sin. A week later it returned with vengeance after she fell out with her daughter and spoke bitter words of judgement to her. Unforgiveness was clearly the root. It turned out she had many people to forgive. She had been previously healed under the extravagant mercy of God, but it returned because she had allowed unforgiveness back in her heart. When I invited her to let go of this unforgiveness, she wasn't willing. She would rather hold onto bitterness and hatred and suffer pain than forgive and experience healing and peace in her heart. I was stunned by her reaction and more so by the gracious mercy of God to forgive and heal her without any former repentance.

Jealousy
Jealousy is a poison. Jealousy can either affect the person who harbours the jealousy, or affect the person whom they feel jealous towards. It can hinder you in your personal growth and ministry. Everyone may feel jealous of someone at some point in time, especially when someone is shown favour or has something you

want or can't have. Jealousy causes negative words to flow from the tongue. We are to repent of a jealous spirit the moment we recognise it, and choose to cheer the other person on or genuinely congratulate them. Instead of allowing any jealousy in our hearts, we can choose to pray a blessing over them and thank God for them. We are to deal with our own issues first, such as a competitive spirit, the need to be approved or the need to be the centre of attention. These are symptoms of an orphan heart that we can surrender to the Lord as we find our acceptance and affirmation in Him.

Sometimes, the spirit of jealousy may be so strong in someone that it may obstruct another person's ministry. This is when jealousy has developed into a form of witchcraft. In such cases, we may require further ministry to be freed from the effects of another person's jealous spirit and this may require us to present the case before the courts of heaven (for more read in Volume 3 *'Accessing the Courts of Heaven'*). One of the ways to oppose a jealous spirit is to choose to honour one another.

Forgiving Self

Some people may be able to forgive others but struggle to forgive themselves. In such cases, there may be self-hate and self-rejection linked to unforgiveness. When a person carries self-hate and self-rejection in their heart, they may avoid looking in a mirror for they don't like what they see. There are various ways we can forgive ourselves. First, we are to realise that if Jesus is willing to forgive us, then we are to forgive ourselves, no matter how bad the sin may seem. If we don't, then in effect we are punishing ourselves and may inflict pain or sickness on ourselves as a result. Some people may struggle to forgive themselves especially if they have made a vow to never forgive themselves. This vow is to be broken in order for the person to forgive themselves.

One of the ways to self forgive is by saying your name followed by *'I forgive you for ... I no longer hold this against you...I no longer blame you or am ashamed of you...I break all word-curses I have spoken over you....I choose to love you.'* Take time and say it as many times as needed until you have forgiven yourself. Sometimes, it takes more than once to say it, in order for it to penetrate deep in our heart. If that doesn't seem to work, then look in a mirror and say the words again but look into you own eyes as you do. This usually works, when the words are spoken from the heart.

There is another way which is powerful and involves addressing areas of self-rejection and self-hate in your heart. There may be a part of your heart which is wounded and you have rejected through self-hate. You can speak directly to this part of your heart by saying you are sorry for rejecting and hating it, for you didn't know how to handle the pain, and then bring this wounded part of your heart to Jesus. This is a way of accepting this rejected part of your heart back again, through connecting the hurt emotion with Jesus. (This is discussed in more detail in *'Divine Heart Surgery'* Chapter 9: *Healing and Freedom From Abuse*.)

Judgement

There are three areas of judgement; *God the Judge, righteous judgement,* and *unrighteous judgement.*

God our Judge.
Most of us are quick to judge especially if there is something we don't like or if people offend us. However, God is the One and only Judge who judges all people. *'Anyone who speaks against his brother or judges him, speaks against the law and judges it. There is only one Lawgiver and Judge, the One who is able to save and destroy. But you- who are you to judge your neighbour?'* (James 4:11-12).

Sometimes, it may be right to approach God, as our Judge, in the Courts of Heaven, especially when an issue requires divine action or intervention (Hebrews 12:23). Job, Solomon and David, each presented their 'cases' to God in the Courts of Heaven (Job 9:15, 13:8, Psalm 72:1+2, 26:1).

Jesus refers to God as our Judge in the parable of the persistent widow with the unjust judge. He told this parable to encourage us to persist in prayer. He said: *'And will not God bring about justice for His chosen ones, who cry out to Him day and night? I tell you, He will see that they get justice, and quickly,'* (Luke 18:7-8). Knowing how to present cases in the Courts of Heaven is a valuable tool and is discussed further in Volume three.

Righteous Judgment

Righteous judgment refers to us doing what is right in the eyes of the Lord. This means we see as He sees, and discern His truth and wisdom in each case or situation. This is clearly outlined through the prophet Isaiah: *'He will not judge by what he sees with his eyes, or decide by what he hears with his ears; but with righteousness he will judge the needy, with justice he will give decisions for the poor of the earth,'* (Isaiah 11:3-4). To walk in righteous judgment requires the seven-fold Spirit of God: *the Spirit of Wisdom and Understanding, the Spirit of Counsel and Power, the Spirit of Knowledge and the Fear of the Lord*. And God releases this in the hearts of those who pursue Him and abide in His Presence: *'The Spirit of the Lord will rest on him'* (Isaiah 11:2).

Self-righteous Judgment

Self-righteous judgment is judging others through our own eyes and self-opinion. This can lead us into emotional or spiritual bondage. Jesus said: *'Do not judge or you too will be judged. For in the same way you judge others, you will be judged, and with the measure you use, it will be measured to you,'* (Matthew 7:1-2). We may falsely believe we have a right to judge others, especially when they are in the wrong or have offended our pride in some way. The danger is we start accusing them and building up toxins in our body, full of self-righteous anger and a critical spirit. Hence, we are to recognise this and instead choose to forgive. It's important to let go of any anger, criticism or judgment and ask God for the right way to respond in every given situation. James said: *'Be quick to listen, slow to speak and slow to become angry, for man's anger doesn't bring about the righteous life that God desires'* (James 1:19).

Why Do We Judge?

Whenever we speak with a judgmental attitude, we are actually putting others down and elevating ourselves. Hence, self-righteous judgment makes us feel better or elevated above others. It empowers self and is full of self-opinion and pride of knowledge, or a sense of being superior to others. When we speak critical words, we may judge others because we feel intimidated by others. If we judge with a negative or critical spirit, the spirit of judgement blocks us from wanting to pray or intercede for the person, and distances us from God's Presence. We usually have to calm down and repent of our wrong attitude before we can pray for the other person.

The truth is we have no right to judge with an unrighteous, self-opinionated or condemning spirit. God is the One who is the Judge. We are to choose to love, forgive and pray for those who irritate, hurt or frustrate us. Scientific studies have shown it takes around four weeks to create a new wire or pathway in the brain and to disenable a toxic pathway. So if we have harboured or rehearsed thoughts of jealousy, judgment, resentment and so on, we are to stop feeding this pathway with such toxic, negative thoughts. This means we no longer feed it with the critical thoughts, but learn to pray blessings for the person or keep forgiving them and try to see them as the Lord does. This also applies to harbouring negative thoughts about ourselves. Instead of speaking or thinking such negative thoughts, we can thank God for creating us in His image and ask Him how He sees us.

We can ask God for daily filters for our heart and mind, so we don't react as the world does to people's mistakes or ongoing issues, but see them as the Lord wants us to and be immune to judgement. If we judge, then we will be judged. Hence, Jesus told us to pray for our enemies and for those who persecute us.

Heaviness in Heart

Judgment and unforgiveness usually produce a sense of heaviness in the heart. After teaching on forgiveness, a Sudanese pastor decided to forgive his so-called friend who had stolen a lot of money from him. For years he had been trying to track his friend and demand he gave back what he owed. Then he decided to let his friend off the hook and no longer demand it back, but tell him he owed him nothing. By the grace of God he was able to do this and felt a heavy weight leave his shoulders as soon as he forgave him from his heart. He wasn't aware of the heavy chains he had been carrying that were like a weight on his back, until he forgave. These were the chains full of bitterness, hatred, anger, revenge and judgement. He was smiling with a sense of freedom and joy in his heart, and chose to turn to God to help him with his financial loss.

Forgiveness brings inner peace and freedom as we release ourselves from the heavy chains that have kept us in bondage. Since God is a God of justice and righteousness, He will help us as we turn to Him for justice. A vital key is to forgive from the heart.

Steps to Freedom from Bondage

Here are the steps to release forgiveness in our hearts.

Break any Vows to Never Forgive

Some people may struggle to forgive because they have made a vow to never forgive others or themselves. This ungodly vow was made in anger, hurt and pain and acts like a bolt on the door of the heart until it is broken. We break the vow *to never forgive*, in the name of Jesus. There was a Ugandan pastor who couldn't forgive and didn't know why he had a blockage in his heart. I asked him if he had ever made a vow in anger to never forgive. He confessed he had and was willing to break this vow, in Jesus' name. After the vow was broken, he was able to forgive a certain person and restore his relationship with them.

Forgive From Your Heart– a) Yourself b) Others or c) God.

Forgiveness applies to ourselves, others or God. God is never in the wrong so in theory we don't need to forgive Him. However, some may feel disappointed with God or blame Him for the things that happened. If so, it is good to tell God what we feel in our hearts towards Him and then give Him our negative feelings.

To forgive from the heart we can imagine our offender(s) standing in front of us. Then look into their eyes and say something to them like this:
- *I forgive you (name)....... for ..... (and name all the offenses).*
- *I no longer hold this against you.*
- *I choose to no longer judge you.*
- *I let you off the hook, you owe me nothing!*
- *I release you to Jesus*

Release each person by handing them to Jesus. And then pray a blessing for the person(s), for this will release more healing and freedom in your heart (eg pray for their salvation or healing).

Once we have forgiven from our heart, there is usually a sense of relief, or tears, or a deep sigh. And instead of feeling grudges, heaviness, hate, or anger, there is a sense of lightness and inner peace.

Let Go of the Toxins (negative emotions)
Next, we can release every toxin we have been carrying in our heart, such as resentment, judgment, jealousy, criticism, hatred, revenge and bitterness. It is time to let these toxic thoughts and feelings go by giving them to Jesus. As we do this, we can renounce any ungodly spirits attached to these negative emotions.

Receive Cleansing & Forgiveness.
Now we can ask the Lord to cleanse our hearts and body with His blood, as we receive His forgiveness. For some, it may help to imagine yourself standing under a waterfall or being immersed in a pool of water and then being cleansed as you allow all the negative feelings and toxins to be washed away. This only takes a minute to do with a sanctified imagination, and is a powerful way to release our negative emotions in exchange for His peace.

Receive His Heart for the Person(s)
Finally, how does the Lord want us to respond to the person(s) if we should see them again? (This may not apply in some cases, especially if the person is deceased). Or we can ask Jesus how He sees the person(s). This helps us to see the person from the Lord's perspective with the right attitude of heart.

Sometimes, Jesus may heal instantly, without needing to verbalise all the above, when He sees our hearts. This happened to the man who hung on the cross next to Jesus. The thief looked into Jesus' eyes and with a repentant heart said: '*Jesus, remember me when You come into Your Kingdom,*' and Jesus replied: '*Today, you will be with Me in Paradise*' (Luke 23:42-43). This was a heart to heart, spirit to Spirit encounter, where Jesus responded to this man's heart and instantly forgave him for his sins.

Forgiveness is a powerful weapon to unlock our hearts from bondage and help us walk in healing and freedom, especially when we learn to forgive from the heart on a regular basis.

7

Generational Sins & Familial Spirits

Rabbi, who sinned, this man or his parents, that he was born blind?

John 9:2

Generational sins, also known as 'ancestral sins', or 'sins of the forefathers', are the sins inherited from our parents, grandparents and previous generations. In the same way we can inherit good genes and blessings from our parents and ancestors, so we can inherit unhealthy genes and curses due to unconfessed sins. Generational sins can apply to churches, nations and royal bloodlines, where sins can be passed from one leader to the next and subsequently affect a church or nation.

Generational sins or the sins of our ancestors can present in the form of recurring illnesses, financial issues, family curses or ongoing problems. When we have inherited the same issues from our parents or grandparents, then the condition is likely to be a generational sin. Generational sins also carry curses. Hence, when something is seen to repeat itself down the bloodline (though sometimes a generation may be skipped), then it may be due to a curse from a door open to sin somewhere in the bloodline.

Some Christians believe we are not affected by generational sins and curses, because generational sins are dealt with at the cross the moment we become a Christian. How I would love this to be true, but it is clear in scriptures how we are affected by the sins of our forefathers, and this usually requires repentance and forgiveness for each of the sins. Being saved is simply the entry point in our journey of salvation. Over time, God reveals the various enemy strongholds that have been at work in our life. Most strongholds have probably been passed down the bloodline from our parents and forefathers. The good news is the blood of Jesus can break off every generational curse and cleanse us from all generational sin. We no longer have to live in bondage as a result of the sins and curses of our forefathers, but can be set free through the power of His blood. We simply forgive our forefathers and ask God to forgive us for each of the various sins.

Jesus addressed the sins of our forefathers: *'Woe to you, teachers of the law and Pharisees, you hypocrites! You build tombs for the prophets and decorate the graves of the righteous. And you say, "If we had lived in the days of our forefathers, we would not have taken part with them in shedding the blood of the prophets". So you testify against yourselves that you are the descendants of those who murdered the prophets.* **Fill up, then, the measure of the sin of your forefathers***!'* (Matthew 23:29-32).

Peter said we were redeemed from the sins of our forefathers through the precious blood of Jesus. '*For you know that it was not with perishable things like silver or gold that you were redeemed from* **the empty ways of life handed down to you by your forefathers,** *but with the precious blood of Jesus, a lamb without blemish or defect,*' (1 Peter 1:18-19).

Also, the disciples questioned Jesus if the man born blind was blind as a result of his own sins or the sins of his parents. Jesus replied by saying neither. He wasn't disagreeing with what they were saying, but that it wasn't the reason for this man's blindness. If a generational sin wasn't possible, Jesus would have commented on this to the disciples, but He didn't. He was agreeing that it could happen though it wasn't the case for this man's blindness (John 9:1-3).

One African lady testified (after praying through a list of known generational sins and curses) that when it came to 'addictions', she had an encounter with God. God showed her a band around her wrist and told her it was the band of addiction to alcohol that had been passed down her bloodline. She had authority in Christ to break it off in Jesus' Name. God told her to cut it off her wrist with the authority He had given her. So she did and was set free from any desire for alcohol.

Another lady had suffered ongoing abuse in her family. After she repented and forgave her parents and grandparents, she testified to feeling healed, and like a new born baby.

A pastor had inherited a spirit of oppression from the atrocities that had been committed in his family line through tribal war and conflict, but after prayer and repentance, he was set free. He testified to receiving peace and freedom in his spirit.

While I was visiting a church in Mozambique, the pastor led the whole congregation through a list of ancestral sins. The people wholeheartedly prayed before God as they forgave their ancestors and repented of the sins. Some had tears rolling down their face during the prayers. At the end, when the pastor invited people to come forward to give testimonies, nearly everyone wanted to come. So he only let the first five speak, for there wasn't enough time to hear them all. One lady had been suffering for the past few years with what felt a like a chicken bone stuck in her throat. Her mum had suffered the same and it had come as a result of a curse on the family from a witchdoctor. One of the prayers had broken the curse of witchcraft and the lady was now free from the symptoms. Another lady had packed her bags after a row with her husband, but decided to come to the session. During the prayers, she said she felt something happened inside her, and she no longer wanted to leave her husband. So she called him forward in front of everyone, and said she was happy to get back with him. They kissed and there was shouting as the people clapped on hearing the good news.

So it is true we are affected by the sins of our parents, grandparents and ancestors. If we repent of the sins and forgive our forefathers, then God will forgive us and set us free. We are called to bind up the broken-hearted, proclaim freedom to the captives, release prisoners from darkness, provide the oil of gladness instead of mourning, and to restore the ancient ruins: *'They will rebuild the ancient ruins and restore the places long devastated; they **will renew the ruined cities that have been devastated for generations**,'* (Isaiah 61:4, 49:8). I believe this scripture is referring to the generational sins and curses.

When people identify with the different generational sins and bring them before God, then the curses can be reversed with blessings. Generational sins affect everyone! No-one has a pure and perfect family lineage. Hence, sin continues to be passed from one generation to the next until it is stopped through prayer and repentance. However, the good news is we can exchange any unclean and ungodly lineage that we have inherited down our mother's and father's bloodlines, for God's holy, flawless Kingdom DNA or Godly lineage.

There is no harm, only benefit, when we repent of all the possible inherited sins from our forefathers. Most of the sins we won't know, but as we pray, the Holy Spirit will draw to our attention the sins and curses in our family bloodline. Another way to do this is by praying through a list of known generational sins. As each sin is addressed, we can receive the forgiveness through the power of Jesus' blood.

Though the blood of Jesus can break all curses and cleanse us from all sins, this is not automatically done. We can access His forgiveness for each generational sin through repentant prayer. This can be compared to having money in a bank. The money in our account doesn't automatically come to us. Rather, we access it by putting a debit card in the ATM cash machines. Likewise, Jesus has provided His blood for the forgiveness of sins, but we access it by coming to Him with repentant prayers for each sin.

Jesus took back the keys of death and Hades when He rose from the dead, and now holds the keys to resurrection life (Revelation 1:18). However, these keys don't automatically unlock the doors in our heart that are holding us captive, until we address each area. As we come to Him, He can unlock each door and say, 'Forgiven by My blood, come out and be free.'

Sins Passed down the Churches, Royal Families or Nations
Generational sins may also affect communities, such as a village, church, royal family or even a nation. When it is something affecting a church, royal family, or nation, then a representative from each group can stand in the gap and repent on behalf of their people. This is known as *'Identification Repentance'* prayer or identifying with the sins of a people group and standing in the gap for the people by offering intercessory prayers of repentance.

Nehemiah and Daniel interceded for their people when they identified with the sins of their nation. They stood in the gap between their people and God, and repented for the sins (Nehemiah 1:4-11, Daniel 9:4-19). Instead of receiving ongoing curses, the Israelites could now receive God's blessings, including blessings on finances, crops and health.

There was a famine for three years during King David's reign, so he sought the Lord to find out why. The Lord replied it was due to the sin of his predecessor, King Saul, and his 'blood stained house'. Saul's sin had been passed down the royal blood line to David and brought a famine on the nation. Once David dealt with the sin through repentant prayer, the famine ceased and the land was blessed again with crops (2 Samuel 21:1).

During my time in South Sudan, I was aware of people suffering through famine, displacement and deaths as a result of their corrupt dictator leadership. Tribes were fighting each other over cattle with ongoing tension. Then one man, who was a humble pastor from a tribe in the north, read a book I had by Rev John Mulinde, *'Set Apart For God'* [1] and felt led by God to stand in the gap for his people. He arranged a big gathering for the local churches and government officials to attend and spoke bravely to his people by addressing their issues. The people identified with their sins and wholeheartedly repented before God. There was a shift in the spiritual atmosphere as they did and great rejoicing followed. *'If My people who are called by My name will humble themselves and pray and seek My face and turn from their wicked ways, then will I hear from heaven and will forgive their sin and heal their land,'* (2 Chronicles 7:14).

Some churches or leaders may be under a curse due to the sins of their predecessors. Ungodly covenants or trade deals may have to be annulled. This may be the case if the pastors were freemasons or committed sexual sins. As the sins or ungodly covenants are addressed, the chains can be broken and blessings can be released.

How Far Back do We Pray?

Scriptures outline that sins are passed to the third and fourth generations, or the tenth generation with regards to sexual sins (Exodus 34:6, Deuteronomy 23:2). Hence, we can ask God to cleanse and forgive the sins as far back as fourth generation. Sometimes, it may be that we don't progress in ministry, healings or our relationship with God because of an inherited sin.

One day, I asked the Lord to reveal if there was anything the enemy was holding against me that was blocking my ministry. He revealed some sins that appeared to be far back in the bloodline. For this particular sin, I felt led to bring it before God my Judge and Jesus my Advocate. I repented of the atrocities and sins of my ancestors and asked Jesus to forgive and break off any curse which had come down the blood line. As I prayed, I suddenly had a beautiful vision of Jesus. His eyes were full of mercy, tenderness and love. And He said to my spirit, 'I have been waiting for this'. After I repented and forgave my ancestors, Jesus said, 'Forgiven by My blood'. The case was acquitted. This is the power of Jesus' blood to forgive our sins and speak on our behalf to God our Father and Judge, who can then dismiss the charges that the enemy has brought against us. (More on dealing with Generational sins in the courts of Heaven can be found in the chapter *'Accessing the Courts of Heaven'* in Volume 3).

Familial Spirits

Familial spirits are ungodly spirits that appear familiar because we have grown accustomed to them in our family. This means they are not easily recognized. Because they have become familiar, we assume they are acceptable and normal. We only become aware of such spirits when we recognise they do not follow the ways or character of God, or when the Holy Spirit convicts us of having them. Familial spirits will block us from growing close to God because they conflict with His word and Spirit. Familial spirits may make us gloss over certain words in the scriptures or believe certain scriptures don't apply to us.

I met a woman who was a Christian and leader of a mission team. It turned out she practiced homeopathy, reiki and acupuncture because her mother had taught her this. It was normal practice and she believed it was good. It was also her source of income, until we had a conversation and I challenged her to ask the Lord if He was happy with her doing these alternative practices. So she did and came back to me saying she was convicted and was prepared to renounce what she was doing. The moment she became aware these were ungodly spirits, the other alternative practices she had been involved with were also exposed. Her list of alternative practices was huge, but she was willing to repent. At the end of her prayers, I prayed for the Lord to open the eyes of her heart to learn His ways of healing and for her to minister under the power of His Holy Spirit. As the familial spirits left her inner being, she received the Lord's love and Spirit in return. She looked startled at first as if her mind was recalibrating, but then her face glowed. Her face looked beautiful as she was encountering the awesome Presence and love of God.

Examples of Generation Sins

This list of generational sins is huge since any sin can be passed down from one generation to the next. Whilst I was in South Sudan, teaching on generational sins and curses, I asked the pastors the issues that were seen to repeat down the generations. A prayer list of the generational sins was produced, and included the sins of tribalism, murders, witchcraft, accessing water spirits, premature death, poverty, corruption, sickness and disease, male domination, female slavery, religious spirit, sexual sins and the list goes on.

A prayer guide can be found in Appendix B and modified according to the sins noted in each particular culture. There is a similarity across each culture and some of the frequently occurring sins that apply to all nations include:

- *Poverty spirit, financial issues, or spirit of greed*
- *Fears & Control, manipulation*
- *Addictions*
- *Genetic or recurring illnesses including mental health,*
- *Abuse, sexual sins*
- *Rejection & Abandonment*
- *Occult, Satanism, Witchcraft, Freemasons & Secret Societies*
- *Low self-esteem, insignificance, male or female dominance*
- *Pride & Independent spirit*
- *Barrenness, abortions, premature deaths*

How to Pray
The prayer is straightforward. First, we are to *recognise* the various sins or issues that have come down the bloodline. After this, we can then *repent* for each sin, and *forgive our parents or ancestors* in our mother's and father's bloodline. Next, we ask for the Lord's *forgiveness* since the sin has fallen upon us. Once the sin has been forgiven, we can then *break the curses* attached to the sin, and ask the Lord to *cleanse our bloodline,* through the power of His blood. Finally, we replace the curses with blessings as we *pray blessings* on our families and future generations. So where there has been barrenness in the bloodline, we can pray a blessing for the wombs to conceive. Or where there have been certain illnesses passed down the bloodline, like heart attacks or cancer, we can pray a blessing on this area of health for the present and future generations. Or where there have been any premature deaths, we can pray life to the fullness, and so on.

Unfortunately, it doesn't seem to work the same when we pray a general prayer for all the sins of our forefathers. Rather, we have to address each one specifically as they arise or as the Lord draws each one to our attention. However, God can also be gracious in certain situations and do far more than we ask of Him.

In the case of dealing with repetitive issues or problems that have been passed down from one church leader to another, the present leader can stand in the gap and repent for the sins of his/her predecessors. The sins and curses linked to secret societies, such as freemasonry, are legally binding since they are made under oaths and covenants, and are passed down until they are dealt with through identification repentance prayer. Once there has been repentance and forgiveness, any ungodly spirits and covenants may be renounced and broken. Any curses attached to such sins may then be broken and cleansed through the blood of Jesus, and replaced with a blessing.

How does this affect Our Children?
Some believe that the parent's prayers of forgiveness will cover the sins passed down to their young children. This can be true, though I believe that a child may still inherit the sins of their forefathers unless the parent repents of these sins *before* the child is born. Once a child has been born, the parent can stand in the

gap by praying the same prayers for their child, hence freeing them from any inherited sins. For example, a parent may struggle with anxiety or mental illness and through repentant prayer can break the effects of this curse being passed to their children.

However, if a child is of sufficient age to understand about generational sins, then they can be taught and led in prayer how to forgive the sins of their parents and ancestors. I believe it is good for young adults to pray through the list of generational sins (if this hasn't already been done at a younger age) before they start a family in order to release blessings on their children and future generations.

There was a lady who attended one of my online teaching courses and during the session on Generational Sin and Curses something beautiful occurred. As we were praying through the list of generational sins, her little daughter of around five years of age entered her room. At the same time her daughter entered the room, we were addressing sexual sins including abortion. The lady had tears in her eyes as she repented for her own abortion and forgave her mum for having an abortion. As she broke off the curses linked to abortion, she sensed the Lord was preventing this generational sin from coming upon her daughter. She had tears in her eyes as she shared this testimony.

Sometimes we may have to keep forgiving our parents and grandparents for certain sins or ungodly behavior, especially if they are alive and we are in contact with them. This applies to the sins that are still ongoing and active in the blood-line. Each time we contact a parent or grandparent who is still displaying an ungodly spirit then we are to be careful not to open the door of our hearts to this unclean spirit. This will happen if we judge or criticise them or agree with any negative words spoken by them. This implies we are to forgive them again for their ungodly behavior (be it through negative words or actions towards ourselves or others) and ask God to forgive us and cleanse us with the blood of Jesus from anything we may have acquired or come under while we were with them.

It is good to get in the habit of cleansing the bloodline when ministering healing or freedom, since the majority of issues have probably been passed through the bloodline. (For more information I recommend reading Chester and Betsy Kylstra's 'Restoring The Foundations'[2]).

In some cases, it may be right to approach the courts of Heaven to address specific issues that we have inherited.[3] The Holy Spirit can prompt us when this may be necessary, and we can present the cases before God our Judge and Jesus our Advocate. All demonic influences have to bow down before the Judge of all judges and King of all kings, as they obey God's sovereign commands and decrees. The Lord grants mercy and forgiveness to those who come to Him with repentant and forgiving hearts, and instead of receiving curses, we can now receive His blessings (1 John 1:9, Psalm 32:5, 2 Chronicles 7:14).

END NOTES:

[1] Mulinde, John; *Set Apart For God: The Call to a Surrendered Life; (Sovereign World, 2005)*

[2] Kylstra, Chester; *Restoring The Foundations: An Integrated Approach to Healing Ministry*

Kylstra, Chester: *Biblical Healing and Deliverance; (Chosen, 2007)*

[3] Henderson, Robert; *Receiving Healing From the Courts of Heaven; (Destiny Image 2018).*

8

Connecting Our Hearts to Father God, Jesus and Holy Spirit

I pray...that all of them may be one, Father, just as You are in Me and I am in You. May they also be in us

John 17:21

God created us to have an intimate relationship with Him including knowing Him as our heavenly Father. He sent His One and only Son, Jesus, into the world so that we may know Him and experience life through Him (John 3:17).

Jesus came to overcome the works of the enemy, to redeem us from our sins and to show us the way to the Father. He is our Lord and Saviour, Brother, Friend and Bridegroom King. *'I have come to My garden, My sister, My bride; I have gathered My myrrh with My spice,'* (Song of Songs 5:1).

After His sacrificial death on the cross, Jesus sent the Holy Spirit to be our nurturer, counselor and comforter. The Holy Spirit is like a gentleman, full of grace and truth, who teaches, guides and empowers those who follow Him. Jesus said: *'I will ask the Father and He will give you another **Counsellor** to be with you forever, the **Spirit of Truth**...you know Him for **He lives with you and will be in you**....If anyone loves Me, he will obey My teaching. My Father will love him and **We will come and make our home with him**'* (John 14:17+23). These verses clearly refer to the Trinity dwelling in us. However, some may find it easy to relate to Jesus but not to

Father God. And others may relate more to the Holy Spirit instead of to Jesus. The truth is we were created to relate to all three.

Just before Jesus faced the cross, He prayed a most passionate prayer to His Father: *'I pray...that all of them may be one, Father, just as You are in Me and I am in You. May they also be in Us... I have given them the glory that You gave Me, that they may be one as We are One: I in them and You in Me'* (John 17:21-23). Jesus said this powerful prayer so we may have the same relationship with the Father as He does, and this includes experiencing and sharing in His glory. His glory is His manifest Presence. This is the most intimate relationship we could ever have with Father God, Jesus and the Holy Spirit: to be one with Him, where He is in us and we are in Him. This is perfect union with God. It is ecstatic love, for God is love. It is beyond words or description, for it is abiding in His manifest Presence. This is our quest in life, to reach this place of communion with Father God, Jesus and Holy Spirit, so we may dwell in Him and He may dwell in us.

God knows every issue and blockage in our heart that prevents us from communing with the Trinity. However, He wants to unblock these areas, so we may connect our hearts to the heart of the Father, Jesus, and Holy Spirit, and enjoy an ongoing intimate fellowship and communion with all three.

Healing the Relationships with our Dad, Mum & Siblings

One of the tools I have adapted to help restore relationships with the Trinity is known as the *'Father Ladder'*[1] from Bethel Sozo Ministries. This tool helps to unblock and re-connect our hearts to the heart of Father God, Jesus and the Holy Spirit, in a relatively simple way. However, once our hearts have connected to Father God, Jesus and Holy Spirit, the next step is to pursue a relationship with all three by spending time devouring His word and engaging with His Presence on a regular basis.

This applies to any new relationship because a relationship depends on the desire to get to know someone, and this involves spending time with them. The choice is up to us. How intimate do we want to be with the Trinity? God has so much to reveal to our hearts, but this comes from pursuing a relationship with Him.

Our relationship with our natural fathers (or male authoritative figures) will influence how we see God as our Father. Those who have had a good relationship with their natural father will find it easy to relate to God as their heavenly Father. However, anyone who has had a poor or abusive relationship with their natural father, or lacked having a father figure, may struggle to see God as their heavenly Father.

The first time I heard about the 'Father Heart of God' was at a Discipleship Training School with Youth With A Mission in my late teenage years. For myself, I found it easy to see God as my heavenly Father because I had a loving relationship with my natural father. However, there was a man in the school who cried out, 'How can God love me as a Father?' He was angry and hurt, because he had never received love from his natural father. Instead, he had been abused and beaten as a child, so he struggled in believing God could love him as a Father. Once he forgave his natural father from his heart and released all the toxic emotions to Jesus, his heart was able to encounter the unconditional love from the Father's heart.

In a similar way, if a person has had a difficult or abusive relationship with their siblings, friends, or girlfriends/boyfriends, then they may struggle to have a relationship with Jesus. Jesus is initially seen as a brother when we are adopted as sons and daughters in God's family. However, as we further grow and mature in the Spirit, our relationship with Jesus changes from seeing Him as a brother, to a friend (John 15:14-15) and finally as our Bridegroom-King. This is when He invites His bride (the body of Christ) to enter into a covenantal relationship with Him (see Ezekiel 16:8, Revelation 19:7-9).

Likewise, people who experienced a poor relationship with their mother (or maternal authority figures) as a result of abuse, rejection, or lack of love, may struggle connecting to the Holy Spirit. The Holy Spirit is seen as our nurturer, counselor and comforter (John 15:26). These qualities are usually received from the mother, but can also be received from the father. Likewise, some of the qualities we receive from our natural father we may receive from our mother, especially with regards to single parent families.

Any issues we had with our natural father, siblings/friends, and mother, may require healing in order to connect our hearts with Father God, Jesus and the Holy Spirit respectively. This is a beautiful example of how healing and sonship go together. As we let God heal our hearts of rejection, emotional wounds or areas of abuse, our relationship with Him can start to grow and flourish. He loves healing and restoring hearts, so we may grow in a deeper relationship with Him. And as we grow deeper, we will discover more of our true identity as His sons and daughters.

Heart of the Father

Some people may have never had a father, either because their father died or they never knew him. For others, the father was never around because he worked long hours, or if he was around, he may have neglected them by giving them minimal physical or emotional attention. In other cases, the father may have been present but abusive to his children, either physically, emotionally (verbally), sexually, or spiritually. Or some fathers may have shown 'conditional' love, where they displayed love only when the child met their needs or did what they wanted. Conditional love is more performance orientated where it is based on reaching goals or standards, and only when a child meets the father's expectations do they receive love. For example, the father may only show love to the child if they obtain high grades in all their exams, or reach the goals the father expected them to reach. The child feels they are never good enough for their father and a sense of failure even when they do well. Some fathers may seem to be only interested in their own needs and not the child's needs. Some of these issues with regards to a father's heart may apply to a mother's heart too.

Then there are those who were brought up by a good father, or the father who loved them unconditionally. This means they are loved for *who they are* and not *what they do*. The good father is one who plays with the child and spends time with them because he wants to. The good father affirms his child as his son or daughter and loves them equally. He is one who protects and provides for his child and is there for them when needed.

However, no father is perfect, and some may struggle with having to please the good father or never let the father down.

It is not uncommon to see the same behavior repeat itself down the blood-line. Unless we forgive our parents and receive healing from God, we are at risk of treating our children the same way that we were treated. Many parents fail to love because of the way they were brought up by their parents.

There was a man who was desperate to be loved by his own father. His father was unable to demonstrate any kind of love to him, or even say the words 'I love you, son'. During a time of ministry, this man received the revelation that his father was unable to love for his grandfather didn't love his father, and a 'lack of love' had come down the blood-line. As he forgave his natural father for not loving him during the various times of his life, his heart became opened to receive Father God's unconditional love. He was overwhelmed with tears as He received the Father's love and saw himself as a little boy holding Father God's hand. He felt accepted, wanted, cherished and loved for simply being an adopted son of the Father.

We have only one perfect Father and that is the heart of our heavenly Father. Father God will never leave or reject us. He is for us and not against us, and will answer when we call on His name. His love is unconditional and this means we don't have to *do* anything to earn it. All it requires is for us to simply *be* his child. John Arnott (Founder of Catch The Fire, Toronto) said, *'He loves us just the way we are but loves us too much to leave us the way we are'* (Psalm139:13-14). God has the best plans for us and has given us the free will to follow Him or not. He speaks the truth in love and disciplines us with love, and forgives when we earnestly repent. He is the most generous Father and is there to protect us as we choose to follow and obey Him. And when we rebel or disobey Him, He waits for our hearts to return to Him (Luke 15:20). His love for us never changes, but we are the ones who change as we open our hearts to Him.

Role of the Father

The love we receive from our natural fathers is meant to be a role model of our heavenly Father's love with regards to our *Identity,*

Provision and Protection. The father is usually the one who provides, protects and helps nurture our identity as a son or daughter. (This is not to say that the mother can't provide, protect or help nurture a child's identity). If our father fails to nurture in these areas, then we may struggle with our true identity, and find it difficult to see God as our Father, provider, and protector.

Sometimes, there may be other male authoritative figures that take on the father's role, such as a grandfather, uncle or teacher, or someone who played a key role in the child's life. In some cases, the father figure may have loved and affirmed the son or daughter, yet failed to provide or protect. Or they may have provided, but failed to protect or display any love. Each of these areas can be specifically addressed in the healing of hearts.

Identity

Sons and daughters usually gain their identity, including their sexual identity, from a healthy relationship with their father. This includes the need for acceptance and belonging. Our worldly identity is based on what we do and many struggle with their identity when they lose their job or retire from work. However, our true identity is related to how our heavenly Father sees us and not what we do. Our work or ministry isn't our identity but an assignment.

Acceptance

The good father accepts his child with an unconditional love. There is nothing they need to do to earn His love. It was there from the moment of conception, and will always be there for them. He is there for them and makes time to be with them. This is not because he has to, but because he wants to. He enjoys laughing, having fun and simply being with His son or daughter. The relationship is pure, transparent and loving, and there is Godly discipline where needed.

God our Father disciplines us as His children for our good, so we may share in His holiness (Hebrews 12:10). After Jesus was baptized in the river Jordan, the Father said to Him: *'You are My Son, whom I love; with You I am well pleased,'* (Luke 3:22). Jesus had done nothing to earn or deserve His Father's love. He simply was His Father's Son, and that is all that mattered. Father God said this *before* Jesus entered His full-time ministry. We are accepted simply because we *are* His son or daughter, and made in His image, not by anything we do. What we do on earth isn't our identity but our assignment.

While I was on the mission field with Iris Ministries the Lord challenged me about my true identity. My identity had become attached to the work I did as a doctor since everyone called me by the name 'Dr Ange'. Until one day Father God put this right. It was during a time of corporate worship when the Father lovingly asked me to give Him my hat. He was spiritually referring to me wearing a hat with the name Dr Ange. I reluctantly took off my hat and gave it to Him. Next, He spoke these words to my heart: *'Ange, I do not see you as a **doctor**, but My **daughter!**'* He gave me the revelation that the work I do for Him is my assignment and not my identity and I was not to confuse my work with my true identity.

An orphan heart strives *to be* accepted and loved, whereas a heart of sonship works *from* a place of acceptance and love. Acceptance includes feeling significant and valued as a son or daughter and not needing to prove yourself to anyone.

Belonging
With our identity comes a sense of belonging. The father makes his children feel they belong to him. They are uniquely made. There is a special bond and relationship between the father and son or daughter. This special bond with the father is an important bond in the child's life. He affirms them as His son or daughter by loving them in the appropriate ways. He appreciates and values them. All future relationships can be developed from this deep sense of belonging. Hence, the child doesn't have to search for belonging in other relationships, because they know where they belong. Belonging includes feeling a sense of comfort and security, and affirms our identity. Father God has created us all to belong to Him: *'Little children, you can be certain that you belong to God'* (1 John 4:4 TPT). *'One will say 'I belong to the Lord''* (Isaiah 44:5).

There was a lady who had an abusive upbringing and as a result she felt an anger and resentment towards her parents. I led her to forgive her father and mother for their verbal and physical abuse. She forgave them as she spoke from her heart words of forgiveness to each of them. Then she let go of her toxic emotions and gave them to Jesus. After receiving an inner cleansing with the blood of Jesus, she encountered the Father's unconditional love for the first time in her life. As she embraced His amazing love she said these words with a peace in her heart: 'I've come home. I know where I belong!' Father God revealed to her heart her true belonging.

Sexual Identity
The father relates to his child as his son or daughter in a special way. He allows special father/son and father/daughter moments, by hanging out and having fun with them. He provides moments to just be together and share heart to heart. He makes them know how proud he is of them, simply because *they are* his son or daughter. Hence, the child's mind, heart and spirit, knows their father loves them and appreciates them. The father's love and ongoing support provides a strong base for their identity.

Sons and daughters are equal in Father God's sight, because He loves us and created us in His image. His children are loved with the same unconditional love, and given the same amount of attention and favour. Worldly culture may view men as being superior to women or vice versa, but Father God sees us as equal.

Provision
The father is usually the one who provides for the family, though in some cases it may be the mother, or both. The child usually never lacks anything they need. This includes a home, food, clothes, money when needed, holidays and the general things in life. A relationship of trust is developed, as they learn to ask their father for things, and know he will provide where needed. There is a dependency on the father to provide and look after their needs. A loving father provides the best for his children, for he wants them to enjoy life to the fullest. Sometimes he may provide without them asking, for it gives him pleasure to do so. And if he doesn't provide, then there is a reason for this. Not everything the child may want may be good for them.

Father God wants us to develop this child-like faith and trust in Him as we ask Him for things. If it pleases Him, He will give us the things we ask for, sometimes immediately and other times we may have to wait. He is a generous Father and we can ask Him for the things we need on a regular basis, not from an orphan heart but a sonship relationship. Many times I have asked Father God to provide for me and He has lovingly done so, when it has been pleasing to Him and in accordance with His will. You may think God doesn't provide for you but have you asked Him? Jesus said: *'Ask and it will be given to you...how much more will your Father in heaven give good gifts to those who ask Him!'*(Matthew 7:7-12).

Protection
The father is the one who protects the family because he is usually the strongest. He carries authority as head of the family. He protects his children when they are with him, but will also rescue and help them when they are hurt, lost or in trouble. He guards and watches over them until they are old or mature enough to take care for themselves. Children feel safe and secure when the father is around. They trust him to protect them from harm or danger. They don't fear anything if they know their father is there, because they feel very secure and safe in their father's presence.

However, if we didn't feel protected by our natural fathers then we will think that God will not protect us. We will struggle to put our trust in God and think we must protect ourselves or seek protection from others. As we forgive our natural fathers for not protecting us, we can ask the Father what He wants to say concerning this. As we believe His words of truth spoken in love, we can start to trust Him with everything in our life.

I was out walking in the local forest when I noticed a young boy of around five years of age walking with his father in the depths of the forest. They were holding hands and though the little boy had no clue where they were or where they were going, he felt safe and secure with his father and that was all that mattered. This is the same child-like faith and trust that our Heavenly Father wants us to have with Him as we hold his hand not knowing where we are going. The safest place to be is in His Presence.

Symptoms of Lack of the Father's Love

In some cases, the natural father may have affirmed the child as his son or daughter but failed to provide or protect when needed. Or he may have been able to provide but not developed a loving relationship with his son or daughter. Sometimes, a father may say the right words, but lack the emotional demonstration in his heart or not be able to keep his promises. Here are some issues we may encounter from a lack of the father's love.

Struggle with Identity
When there has been a lack of the father's love expressed through words, emotions or actions, we may struggle with our identity. There is usually a sense of rejection or low self-worth, and the need to seek acceptance, belonging, love and security in other relationships. Some may feel a sense of self-hatred because they are not good enough, or not wanted, or especially if there has been abuse. Those who have received abuse from the father may be drawn to abusive relationships, or at risk of abusing others. Some may seek alternative sources to meet their emotional needs, such as drugs, alcohol, sex, money or pornography. Others may struggle with depression to the point of self-harm or attempted suicide. Many will admit they don't know who they are, or their identity is in their job or relationship with others.

Lack of Protection
Usually, when a father has failed to protect his child, or not been around when the child needed him, the child may be prone to anxiety, fear or panic attacks. They may struggle with insecurity, especially when alone. They develop the belief that they need to protect themselves for no-one else will, and may go about this in various ways. Some may have made a vow that they don't need anyone and can protect themselves. Others may seek protection or security in relationships, or possessions. They may struggle with letting God protect them, because they think He will let them down just as their father did.

Lack of Provision
Where there has been a lack of provision by the father, the child may struggle to trust in God to provide for their needs or think He doesn't care for them. They may be anxious about their finances, or live with a fear of never having enough. Some may look to others as a source of provision, or become self-sufficient and independent of others but still struggle with a poverty spirit.

Dealing with the Symptoms

Each of these three areas, *identity, provision and protection* can be dealt with by forgiving the natural father wherever he failed in these areas. There are usually many negative thoughts and false beliefs concerning a person's views about Father God, and these can each be exchanged by asking Father God for His truth.

Each area of hurt, pain or false belief, can be addressed in turn. One way to do this is for the person to imagine their natural father standing in front of them and then to speak directly with the words they've wanted to say to him. The words can then flow from the person's heart.

Once the person has forgiven their natural father (or father figure) for the various things that hurt them, they can give their toxic emotions to Jesus (eg anger, resentment, judgment, hatred, bitterness etc). Next, they can break any ungodly soul-ties with their father or father figure (soul-ties are discussed in Chapter 11).

Now they are ready to receive inner cleansing and this may be done by imagining themselves (with the sanctified imagination) under a divine waterfall. Cleansing is received as the sanctified water of the Holy Spirit washes over them. Their hearts are cleansed and purified as the toxic emotions (including defilement) are released to the cross. As we pray for all the negative emotions to be washed away by the blood of Jesus, we cleanse their body, soul and spirit, especially their body memory, cognitive memory, emotion memory and spirit memory. This usually takes just a few minutes.

Jesus came to show us the way to the Father and to reveal the Father's heart to us. He said: *'No-one comes to the Father except through Me'* (John 14:6). Hence, we can ask Jesus to reveal the Father's heart. This is a special moment where the person can hear what Father God wants to say to them as they encounter His loving Presence. I encourage the person to ask Jesus to reveal the Father or ask the Father to reveal His unconditional love to them. Some may see themselves with Father God, others may receive intimate words from Him or encounter His love in their hearts. I may ask the person, *'What do you see the Father doing, or what does He want to say?'* Or I may get the person to ask, *'Father, how do You see me? What do You want to say?'* In some cases I may ask the Father, *'Father, what do You want to say?'* And, *'Father, what do You want to do, or give them?'* Many receive His truth concerning how He sees them, and how He thinks about them. Some see themselves sitting on the Father's lap, others playing with the Father or holding His hand. Some see brilliant light and others sense a Father's embrace. It will be different for each person. This is powerful when it is experienced firsthand by the person. It releases healing to their emotions along with a fresh revelation of the Father's love for them.

Sometimes, I may feel led by the Spirit to prophetically minister to a person's heart, as if the Father is speaking directly to them. These words carry His love and power as they flow from the heart of God.

I met a woman who felt depressed and suicidal as a result of the hurt and rejection she had received from her father. She longed to be loved by him, but he was unable to love her in the way she needed. He failed to provide for her and protect her and was never there when she needed him. She felt confused with her identity and had reached the point where she wanted to end her life, even though she was married with children. She had believed the lies that Father God wasn't interested in her or didn't have time for her.

I led her through the process of forgiveness, where she imagined her dad standing in front of her and one by one, forgave him for all the things he did that caused her pain or where he failed her. She cried as she forgave him. She let him off the hook and told him he owed her nothing. She wasn't going to hold this against him anymore. She prayed for him to know Jesus and Father God and spoke a blessing over him, and she chose to honour him, simply for being her father. Next, we broke the ungodly soul-ties between her and the father, and then she received the inner cleansing as all the pain, rejection, anger, and other negative emotions were washed and cleansed from her body, soul and spirit through the blood of Jesus. Next, she imagined Father God (with her sanctified imagination) being with her. She sat on His lap, and could enjoy His unconditional love as she felt the Father's warm embrace. She started to laugh and cry, but now with healing and relief. This void in her heart was now overflowing with His unconditional love and acceptance. She heard Him speak His truth, how He saw her and valued His relationship with her. The depression immediately lifted and for the first time in her life she felt excited about what Father God had in store for her. This amazing encounter was just the beginning of her relationship with Father God.

After a corporate session on connecting hearts to the heart of the Father, there was a lady who was healed of a limp in her right leg. During the ministry session, this lady forgave her natural father for abusing her as a child. After forgiving him, she opened her heart to receive love from the heart of the Father. As she walked out of the room, she suddenly felt a click in her right knee. When she heard the click, she knew her knee was instantly healed. At this point, she heard Father God say that as a result of restoring her heart, her walk with Him had been restored. It was an amazing testimony of the body being healed when our hearts are realigned to the Father heart of God. She was glowing with love from the Father.

There was a retired pastor who struggled to connect with the Father heart of God as a result of his abusive upbringing by his father. His natural father failed to say anything good or loving to him throughout his childhood so he never felt loved, appreciated or valued. During the ministry session, he forgave his father for all the things he did, said, or failed to do. When it came to encountering the Father heart of God, I encouraged him to write down what the Father was saying to his heart. As he wrote down the words, he realized there were no negative words but all the words were positive. It was amazing what the Father revealed to his heart as He invited him into a deep relationship of sonship with Him.

Heart of Jesus

The moment we are born-again in God's Kingdom, we become spiritual babies. We can remain as babies or be nurtured to infants and then to little boys and girls. At the early stage of our spiritual growth and development, we are more likely to see Jesus as our brother. However, as we grow and mature in the Spirit we will see Him as our friend (John 15:14). Then a time will come where the Lord will reveal Himself to us as the Bridegroom-King. This will be an invitation to enter into a relationship of betrothal to Him.

Most people see Jesus as their Lord, Saviour, Advocate, Brother, Friend or Bridegroom King. In Song of Songs, the Bridegroom King sees His beloved as His sister and Bride: *'How delightful is your love, My sister, My bride,...you are a garden locked up, My sister, My bride,'* (4:10 + 12). Jesus told His disciples after three and a half years of intimately walking with Him that they were no longer His servants but His friends (John 15:14). However, some may struggle to connect with Jesus as their brother or friend, especially if they had poor or abusive relationships with their siblings or friends during childhood. Or some may struggle to connect with Jesus as their Bridegroom-King if they have been involved in unhealthy sexual or abusive relationships.

There was a woman who struggled to connect with Jesus in her heart. She didn't know why this was the case, and found it easier to pray to Father God and Holy Spirit. So we asked the Lord to reveal if there was any trauma in her past with friends or siblings that He wanted to heal and restore. Immediately, she had a memory of her older brother bullying her. It was a traumatic event. So she forgave her brother for all he did by speaking directly to him as if he was in the room. After this, she welcomed Jesus into this memory. Next, she saw Jesus at the scene of what took place and He was laughing with her. She saw Jesus as her older brother, who loved her and was there for her any time she needed Him. Seeing Jesus in her childhood memory released healing and connected her heart to His.

There was another woman who struggled to connect with Jesus. She knew there was some block in her heart and asked for prayer. The Lord took her back to an experience at school, where she had been bullied by others and felt very much alone. At the time of the bullying, she cried out with pain and *vowed* she no longer needed friends. This was her defense mechanism for her feelings of pain and rejection. She had believed the lie that no-one liked her and that she didn't need anyone. She repented and broke this vow, and then forgave those who bullied her, naming them one by one. Next, she invited Jesus to the scene in the memory. As Jesus stepped into the scene, she began to feel accepted, loved, and saw Him as her true friend. Jesus said He would never leave her and was always there for her. She had found a new friend and the block with Jesus was now removed.

There was a lady who struggled to connect with Jesus because she kept seeing sexual images based on her abusive relationship with her husband. So I led her through forgiving her husband, followed by receiving inner cleansing to her body, soul and spirit. At the end, she felt she had a pure and sanctified heart and could connect her heart to Jesus as her Bridegroom-King.

When we choose to forgive friends, siblings, or sexual partners, for what they did or said, and then invite Jesus into our memories, we will not only receive healing and cleansing, but experience His heart of love and friendship. He will exchange the lies and false beliefs with His Truth. We can ask, *'Jesus, how do you see (name the person)?'* or get the person to ask, *'Jesus, how do You see me?'* Also, we can ask the person, *'What does Jesus think about you, or want to say to you?'* Or the person can ask, *'Jesus, what do You think about me?'* It is powerful as He ministers to our heart and spirit. Many see Jesus as their big brother, friend or Bridegroom-King who is always there for them and enjoys being with them. They realise they will never be alone, for He is always near, especially when they call on His name. *"Because he loves Me,"* says the Lord, *"I will rescue him; I will protect him, for he acknowledges My name. He will call upon Me and I will answer him; I will be with him in trouble. I will deliver him and honor him,"* (Psalm 91:14-15).

Nurturing Heart of the Holy Spirit

Just before His crucifixion, Jesus said that He would send the Holy Spirit: *'If you love me, you will obey what I command. And I will ask the Father, and He will give you another Counselor to be with you forever – the Spirit of Truth…But the Counselor, the Holy Spirit, whom the Father will send in My Name, will teach you all things and will remind you of everything I have said to you'* (John 14: 16 +26). The Greek word for Counselor is *'Parakletos'*[2] and this is a masculine noun that can mean *Advocate, Comforter, Counselor, Teacher* and *Helper.* Jesus said unless He goes away, the Counselor will not come to us, but if He goes, then he can send the Holy Spirit to us (John 16:7-8). And the Holy Spirit will testify about Him and convict us of our sins, as He guides us in all truth (John 15:26, 16:8+13).

Isaiah revealed the nurturing heart of God as he spoke these words from the mouth of the Lord: *'I will extend peace to her like a river, and the wealth of nations like a flooding stream; you will nurse and be carried on her arm and dandled on her knees. As a mother comforts her child, so will I comfort you; and you will be comforted over Jerusalem,'* (Isaiah 66: 12-13, 2 Corinthians 1:3-7). The same prophet spoke these words to God's people: *'For the Lord comforts His people and will have compassion on His afflicted ones. But Zion said, "The Lord has forsaken me, the Lord has forgotten me." Can a mother forget the baby at her breast and have no compassion on the child she has borne? Though she may forget, I will never forget you! See, I have engraved you on the palms of My hands,'* (Isaiah 49:13-15).

Jesus revealed God's nurturing heart: *'O Jerusalem, Jerusalem, you who kill the prophets and stone those sent to you, how often I have longed to gather your children together, as a hen gathers her chicks under her wings, but you were not willing!'* (Luke 13:34).

Sometimes, when a person experiences a negative relationship with their mother, (or substitute female authoritative figure, such as the grandmother, carer, or aunt) they may struggle to engage with the Holy Spirit. This is because the Holy Spirit can be seen as our comforter, helper, nurturer, counselor and teacher. The role of the Holy Spirit is to help guide and counsel us each step of the way, as we choose to live a Spirit-led life.

In such a case, the person is simply to forgive their mother (or female authoritative figure) for past hurts, rejections or abuse (this includes physical, sexual, verbal or neglect). For each wounded emotion or pain, there is usually a lie or false belief attached to the thought. These can be addressed, where each lie or negative thought is given to Jesus, and exchanged for His truth. It is better for the person to ask Jesus for His truth so they may hear it for themselves. He will pop it in their minds when they ask. Once this exchange for the truth has taken place, the recipient can invite the Holy Spirit into their heart. They can also ask for the gift of praying in tongues if they would like to receive this.

I met a woman who was brought up with a controlling and abusive mother. As a result of the ongoing verbal abuse, she had struggled with a fear of rejection throughout her adulthood. Her mother failed to love, comfort, or nurture her. However, the opportunity arose for the Lord to heal her deep emotional wounds. She wept as she forgave her mother for all the things she said or did or failed to do, as the childhood memories came flooding back to her mind. I encouraged her to give to Jesus every lie and word-curse she received from her mum, and ask Him for His truth in exchange. She started to smile when she heard the words of truth from His heart. After she had forgiven and prayed for her mum, we broke the ungodly soul-ties with her mum. This was followed by an inner cleansing as she imagined herself standing under a waterfall. As she gave all her pain to Jesus, she received in exchange the comforting love of the Holy Spirit. Not only that, but she heard the Spirit of God personally speak to her. She discovered how to hear the Holy Spirit as a result of her heart being connected with Him.

God longs to deal with our blockages. These blockages are the result of painful experiences with our father, mother (or male and female authoritative figures), siblings and friends. Through these negative experiences we have believed lies about Him and ourselves. This is why it is not only important to forgive those who have wounded us, but to replace each lie or false belief with the truth God wants us to hear from His heart. Then our hearts can be restored and connected in relationship with the Trinity God. It is then up to us to pursue our relationship with Him. And as we do, we will become more bonded to Him, and learn to trust Him for our provision and protection. Our identity gradually matures as we grow in our relationship with Him, as a brother or sister, a son or daughter, a prince or princess, a friend and ultimately as His bride.

END NOTES

[1] Desilva, Dawna & Liebscher, Teresa: *Basic Sozo Training Manual; Saved, Healed, Delivered.*

[2] Parakletos (3875 Greek): *Strong's Expansive Exhaustive Concordance, Red Letter Edition*

9

Encountering Jesus

He took bread, gave thanks and broke it and gave it to them.
Then their eyes were opened and they recognised Him

Luke 24:30-31

Encountering Jesus is an amazing way to receive healing. This is not surprising since one of Jesus' names is *Jehovah Raphe,* the Lord who heals. One of His assignments was to fulfill what was written in the Book of Isaiah. *'The scroll of the prophet Isaiah was handed to Him. Unrolling it, He found the place where it was written: "The Spirit of the Lord is on me, because he has anointed me to preach good news to the poor. He has sent me to proclaim freedom for the prisoners and recovery of sight for the blind, to release the oppressed, to proclaim the year of the Lord's favour." Then He rolled up the scroll, gave it back to the attendant and sat down. The eyes of everyone were fastened on Him, and He began by saying to them, '"Today this scripture is fulfilled in your hearing,"'* (Luke 4:17-21, Isaiah 61:1-3).

One of the most powerful tools for healing the memories of fears, traumas, abuse, emotional pains and wounded hearts, is to invite Jesus into the painful memory. This can be done with a sanctified imagination. (Remember, in order to have a sanctified imagination we simply surrender our body, soul and spirit to God, and ask Him to cleanse our whole being including the mind, will, emotion, and imagination, with His blood. Then we can pray that our eyes, ears and senses are open to see, hear and sense in the Spirit what the Lord wants to say and reveal to our hearts, as we welcome Him in our hearts by faith).

Most cases of trauma in childhood usually occur before the person becomes a born-again believer. The good news is we can invite Jesus to come into our hearts and heal our trauma memories. He can do this because He is omnipresent (meaning He is everywhere) and outside of time because He is God of the past, present and future. This means we can invite Jesus into any painful memory or traumatic event regardless of when it happened. Our emotions are not connected with time and this means a painful memory can feel as real in the present as it did when it occurred in the past.

When we are struggling with an issue, such as fear, pain, rejection, or disappointment, then we can invite Jesus to minister in this area of our heart. There is usually some root to the emotional symptoms and this may be at the point in time when the symptoms started. Hence, we can ask Jesus to reveal the root or memory when the issue first arose. Some may start to have memories or flashbacks of particular events, as the Lord begins to highlight these wounded areas in the heart. An amazing thing is we can deal with any painful memory when we know His Presence is with us and He is there to help us. Each time we invite Jesus into a scene or memory, we can encounter His power and love in a special way. When Jesus enters a memory we begin to see things in a different light and from a different perspective as He ministers to our hearts.

The memories of a painful or traumatic event are usually stored in the body memory, emotion memory, cognitive memory and spirit memory. This is because our body, mind, emotions and spirit are all affected by shock, pain, fear and trauma. However, our cognitive (or conscious) memory is usually not aware of the pains and wounds stored in our emotion, body and spirit memory, because it has tried to forget or suppress the painful memories. This happens when our conscious mind can't cope with pain or trauma, so it blocks out the emotions in order to survive and get on with daily life. This is a coping and defense mechanism.

Lord take hold of her hand and dance with her. She felt safe as she was in His Presence and this made her willing to walk with Him down memory lane. This time as she revisited her memories, Jesus was right with her and she saw Him turn things around as He ministered healing and freedom in her heart. Finally, she was set free of all fear, shame, blame, and rejection as she gave her wounded emotions to Jesus and welcomed His loving truth in her heart. Though she had some memories of her trauma, she no longer had the pain or wounded emotions attached to it, but could speak about her childhood experiences with peace and freedom in her heart.

Benefits When We Encounter Jesus

Encountering Jesus is powerful and liberating. Experiencing His Presence removes the fears and negative emotions, such as loneliness, isolation, pain and rejection. Suddenly, the lies and fears that are linked to the negative emotions are dealt with as Jesus reveals His truth for every given situation. As the person gives Jesus their negative thoughts, false beliefs and fears, they can ask Him for His truth in exchange. As they hear His words of truth spoken to them in love, they become set free from the lies that have kept them in bondage. This is because Jesus is the Truth and His Truth sets us free (John 8:32). Instead of feeling the pain or trauma, His love, comfort and peace starts to flood through the person's innermost being. Some start to smile and others may laugh with joy. Everyone will have different encounters because Jesus knows exactly how to relate to each one of us. Since He knows our hearts and thoughts, He can minister exactly where needed in our hearts with His healing love and revelatory truth. While some may see in the Spirit, others will sense or hear in the Spirit. Even if the person normally struggles to see, hear or sense things in the spirit, they can still interact with Jesus by faith with a sanctified imagination.

In some situations, where an individual may experience extreme measures of fear or shock in their wounded memory, the person may require rescuing by Jesus from the trauma. In such cases, the Spirit will show us what to do or we can describe what

A painful or fearful memory can be triggered when we experience a similar emotion or painful event. That is why a person may over-react to a minor trigger, because it is tapping into a deep wound or painful memory. People can have sudden bouts of anger or anxiety attacks when a painful emotion is triggered. In such cases, the person is to embrace the painful emotion as they invite Jesus into the memory and receive healing in their heart.

Healing is powerful when Jesus is invited into the scene of a traumatic event or painful memory. When a person invites Jesus into the painful memory, within seconds they usually encounter Him in the scene. As their heart becomes connected to Him, they will begin to receive healing and freedom. This will be different for each person. Some may see or hear in the spirit, whereas others may feel or sense what Jesus is saying and doing.

To encounter Jesus in the memory of a painful event simply requires a sanctified imagination and faith. Most people find it relatively easy to imagine Jesus at the scene of the memory once they have invited Him in. They may see Him as a man in modern clothes or just sense His Presence in the Spirit. If they seem to be struggling to see Him in the Spirit, then I may ask (or get the person to ask) *'Jesus, where are you in this memory?'* The moment they see Him appear I usually ask the person, *'What is Jesus doing or saying?'* Or I may ask Jesus, *'Lord, is there anything You want to do or say?'* Sometimes, when *I* ask such questions, the person may not encounter Jesus. In such cases, I will encourage the *person* to ask Jesus the same questions. I find they usually respond when they ask Him. As their spirit starts to engage with His Spirit, they no longer feel the pain, trauma, fear, isolation or rejection. Healing and freedom can be experienced in their hearts, as they receive His words of comfort, revelation and truth.

In some cases, the Lord will reveal His loving Presence to a person at the start of a session so a person feels safe as if He is holding their hand. When the person is ready, the Lord will take them with Him down memory lane to the scene of the trauma, and minister to their hearts in a personal way.

There was a lady who couldn't face her childhood memories for the trauma pain was too intense and she had blocked the memories. During the ministry session, she felt the we see in the Spirit, as Jesus comes in the memory and rescues the person. This is a form of *prophetic healing and deliverance*. Prophetic healing and deliverance is where the facilitator can see or hear in the Spirit what the Lord is saying or doing, and as they speak the words, the person is healed and freed from bondage. After the person has been rescued, then the rest of the healing can continue as they engage with Jesus.

There was a case where a lady was in shock as she froze with fear at the scene of a painful memory. Then I heard the Lord say, 'This is a rescue operation and I will rescue her.' So I described what I saw taking place in the Spirit as the Lord came to the scene, picked up the little girl and took her in His arms into a safe place full of His glory-Presence. The lady said everything I described felt real, as if Jesus had come and rescued her. She was then able to complete the rest of the healing in her encounter with Jesus.

When we encounter Jesus, He will forgive, cleanse and heal our wounded hearts, through the power of His blood that was shed on the cross for us. Hence, part of the healing may include the washing and cleansing from shame, guilt, rejection, fears, defilement, emotional pains, ungodly spirits and negative emotions. Once this is done, Jesus can give us something in exchange for our negative emotions. I ask Jesus if He would like to give the person something. Some may be given spiritual garments that represent purity, righteousness, royalty or belonging. Others are given spiritual gifts or comforting words from His heart. The person receives these as a token of Jesus' love.

Another benefit when we encounter Jesus is that He can show us the way to the Father. He came to reveal the heart of the Father (John 14:8). *'Righteous Father, though the world does not know You, I know You, and they know that You have sent Me. I have made You known to them and will continue to make You known in order that the love You have for Me maybe in them, and that I Myself may be in them,'* (John 17:25). A person may encounter Jesus but not know the Father. Hence, I may ask the person if they want to meet Father God and for Jesus to show them the way to the Father. (Or the person can ask Jesus to reveal the Father's heart or direct them to the Father.)

Paul prayed that the eyes of our heart may be enlightened through His Spirit of wisdom and revelation, and that Christ would dwell in our hearts by faith. *'I keep asking that the God of our Lord Jesus Christ, the glorious Father, may give you the* **Spirit of wisdom and revelation so you may know Him better**. *Also, I pray that the eyes of your heart may be enlightened,* to know the hope to which He has called you, and His incomparably great power for us who believe,' (Ephesians 1:17-19). *'I pray that He may strengthen you with* **power through His Spirit in your inner being**, *so that* **Christ may dwell in your hearts by faith**,' (Ephesians 3:17). This is a prayer we can pray daily.

Healing through Testimonies of Jesus

A testimony is when we give evidence or bear witness to something. This is where the verb 'to testify' comes from. When we testify to the healing power of Jesus, it may also imply 'do it again Lord'.

When we hear about others being healed by Jesus, it stirs our faith to believe He can do the same healing for us, or for those we know who have similar symptoms. Healing can be received from the testimony of another person's encounter with Jesus. When the woman at the well had met Jesus, face to face, she went back to the village to testify to the people about her encounter with Him. Some simply believed Jesus was the Messiah from hearing the words of her testimony. However, others who were encouraged by her testimony wanted to encounter Jesus for themselves, so they went to the well to meet Him. The Samaritans said to the woman: *'We no longer believe just because of what you said; now we have heard for ourselves, and we know that this man really is the Saviour of the world,'* (John 4:42). Our testimonies of encounters with Jesus can encourage others to have a similar encounter with Him.

One of the powerful ways to receive healing is when we hear the testimonies of what Jesus did for someone else. What Jesus did for one, He can do for another. We simply are to believe He will meet us as we open our hearts by faith to Him.

Heart to Heart Ministry

The most precious and unforgettable moments are when we have a heart encounter with Jesus. As we encounter His Spirit, we feel various emotions in our inner being. We may start to feel tearful, repentant or broken inside, or feel our emotions deep within. In these precious moments, we may say few words, but our heart feels everything. In His love and mercy, He pours His grace and forgiveness in our hearts, and our tears of sadness or remorse are turned into thankfulness and joy. This is a heart to heart moment, as our hearts become connected to the heart of God.

When the man on the cross next to Jesus asked Him to remember him in His Kingdom, Jesus saw this man was full of remorse. This was a heart to heart moment as Jesus saw deeply into the man's repentant heart. He replied, *'Today, you will be with Me in paradise'* (Luke 23:4-0-43). Likewise, the woman who washed Jesus' feet with her tears was releasing her emotions of guilt, shame and sorrows. In this intimate moment, Jesus knew what was going on inside her heart and He forgave her many sins. Her heart was forgiven, healed and transformed during her encounter with Jesus.

Likewise, something similar happened to Peter's heart when he was face to face with Jesus after the resurrection. Peter had denied Jesus three times on the day of the crucifixion and wept bitterly after doing this (Luke 22:60-62). These negative feelings in Peter's heart prevented him from hearing Jesus and drawing close to Him. Peter failed to recognize Jesus' voice when they were out fishing on the Sea of Galilee. It was John, the beloved, who heard and recognized the voice of Jesus and told the others in the boat. The moment John said, 'It is the Lord', Peter jumped into the sea and swam to the shore to meet Jesus (John 21:5-7). Peter needed an encounter with Jesus to restore his relationship and heal his heart. It was then that Jesus ministered to Peter's heart when He asked him three times if he loved Him. In this heart to heart moment, Jesus was healing Peter's heart of bitterness, grief, remorse, pain, guilt and shame. Three times Jesus asked Peter if he loved Him, and each time He was healing Peter's heart of the guilt and shame linked to each denial (John 21:15-18). Jesus was not only healing Peter's heart, but He was reinstating his call to follow Him.

Look Into the Eyes of Jesus

A lady came to me with a feeling of deep emptiness in her heart. She had experienced this before, and described it as a feeling of despair and depression, as if it was coming from a deep void within. As we prayed and asked the Lord to reveal the root or cause for these emotions, she suddenly burst into tears. She cried out loud as she released immense pain from deep within her heart. The pain went back to the memory when her husband left her with the children and never came back. She thought she had dealt with it but the pain was deeply hidden and suppressed in her heart. She couldn't understand why God had allowed this to happen. Deep pain arose from within her heart as she expressed with tears an overwhelming sense of grief. As she was faced down in her deepest pain, I sensed Jesus say 'Get her to look into My eyes'. He wanted to minister directly to her heart. So I invited her to look into Jesus' eyes of love. I said it again, until she lifted up her face from the floor and looked into His eyes of love. As she did, His Spirit ministered to her heart and spirit. Within minutes her tears of pain turned into tears of joy as she started to smile and laugh. She was overwhelmed with His love and compassion. Deep healing took place as she heard Him speak words of love and acceptance to her heart. The void of emptiness disappeared as this area in her heart was healed and filled with the joy and love of Jesus.

Sometimes, I may feel prompted by the Spirit to invite a person to look into the eyes of Jesus. This is powerful especially when a person feels emotionally traumatized or in some form of deep pain. His eyes are described as blazing fire (Revelation 1:14, 19:12). His face is like the sun shining in its brilliance (Revelation 1:16). This is a heart to heart and spirit to Spirit encounter, when we look into the eyes of Jesus. His fiery eyes exude such overwhelming love, mercy and compassion. Healing flows when we look into the eyes of Jesus.

During a training session on *Encountering Jesus*, I invited the Holy Spirit to reveal to the group any hidden painful memories where He wanted to release healing. A woman instantly remembered the scene of a traumatic memory in her childhood. In this memory, she was about six years old when her mum had a heart attack and became unconscious. An ambulance suddenly arrived at the scene to take her mum to the hospital. As a little girl all alone she felt full of fear as her mum was taken from her. So we invited Jesus into the scene of the trauma. Next, she saw Jesus holding her, and she cried as she released her emotions of fear and pain to Him. Then she started to laugh as she felt safe in His loving arms. So I asked Jesus if He wanted to say anything to her, and she heard the words that He will never leave her and is always with her. After this, Jesus fast forwarded her memory to similar scenes when her mum was taken ill again. In each scene, she saw Jesus was there with her and felt such a deep peace after encountering Him in these memories. Jesus wanted to heal these painful memories.

I was driving back from a prayer meeting when a parked Land Rover decided to reverse full throttle at point blank range into the passenger side of my car. My car was thrown to the other side of the road and the passenger side was completely smashed. Though I had no injuries, I was still shaken from the trauma, and suddenly had a fear of driving. I knew I had to deal with these emotions of fear, shock and trauma. So, when I found a moment to be alone with God, I released all the tension and tears from the trauma. Then, I asked Jesus where He was when the car crashed, and why didn't He prevent it from happening? The Lord said He was with me at the scene. He was in the front passenger seat and took the hit as the car smashed into the passenger side. He said it was an attack of the enemy but He protected me from harm, though my car was wrecked. I had a peace in my heart knowing He was with me. After this, I commanded the spirit of fear, shock and trauma that entered during the crash, to leave me in Jesus' Name. Then I faced the fear by immediately driving again. I chose to forgive and pray for the person who drove into my car instead of holding any negative feelings towards her. My car was fully restored and cost me nothing.

Bad things can happen to good people. This verse from Isaiah 43:2-3 stood out after the crash: '***When*** *you pass through the waters, I will be with you; and **when** you pass through the rivers, they* *will not sweep over you. **When** you walk through the fire, you will not be burned. For I am the Lord your God'.*

When we encounter Jesus in traumas, we can give Him our fears, pain or negative emotions, in exchange for receiving His joy, peace and love in our hearts. Jesus can rescue, heal, cleanse and restore our hearts from the painful memories of a trauma or stressful memory, as we invite Him into the memory or scene of the event. He can exchange every fear, lie or negative belief in the memory with His revelatory Truth and love. Jesus came to restore our hearts back to a loving relationship with Him and with the Father.

10

Blessing the Body

*I pray that you may enjoy good health...
even as your soul is getting along well*

3 John 1:2

One of the ways to stay healthy is to bless our body. Without realising, we may speak negative words or agree to the negative words others have spoken, which are in effect curses. Negative words like, 'You can't do this anymore,' 'You will never get better' or 'I always have headaches, stomach problems...' 'I always have this pain and can't do...', 'I will have this for life,' 'I hate my ... part of the body,' 'the doctor said I won't be able to...' and the list of negative thoughts and words goes on.

Likewise, we are to be careful not to abuse our bodies through stress, alcohol, unhealthy food, abusive substances, drugs, or by overdoing it in any way. Otherwise, our bodies may respond back with the symptoms of pain, discomfort, stiffness, tiredness, depression, nervous breakdown, or ill health.

One day, I felt challenged and inspired to bless my body on a regular basis after reading a booklet on healing by Charles Capps[1]. There is power in our words and this means to be careful of what we say. A friend once commented on a casual remark I made and how this comment hurt her. She wanted me to know that my words carried power. I was grateful for her telling me, and realised that I am to guard my tongue and be more careful with my words. The words we speak can either bless or curse. This also applies to the way we see ourselves and what we declare over our bodies. Our bodies respond to our thoughts, words and actions, and also the words spoken by others.

So, I decided to put 'blessing my body' to the test. One day, when I was painting my kitchen, my shoulder and upper back muscles (or *trapezius* muscle) started to ache. I realized I had overdone it, and would probably have upper back pain for the next few days. However, instead of thinking or saying, 'I've overdone it again and will suffer with muscle ache,' I decided to bless my body. I told my shoulder muscles how I was sorry for straining them, and then commanded the acid build up in the muscles to go (lactic acid increases in our muscles during exercise or excess use). As I laid my hands on my muscles, I prayed for the peace and shalom of the Lord to rest on them, and blessed them to have no aches or pains, in the name of Jesus. When I woke up the next morning, I had no aches or signs of stiffness in my body. I was amazed, yet knew this was the power behind blessing my body.

Is My Body Upset with Me?

Sometimes, body pain is simply a cover up of our underlying emotional pain. Maybe we have abused or overused certain parts of our body without realising it. Or maybe we have cursed our body if we do not like it or hate ourselves.

If we are unaware of what we may have done to our bodies, we can ask the Holy Spirit to show us. One way of finding out is to ask the Holy Spirit this question: *'Holy Spirit, have I abused my body in any way?'* If I sense 'yes', then I can ask the Holy Spirit which part of my body, and then say sorry to this part of my body. For example, if I have strained a body part through excessive use, I can say sorry to my body, and then command the pain and inflammation to leave in Jesus' name. Then, I can bless my body to function normal and to receive the peace of the Lord.

Likewise, we can ask the Holy Spirit this question: *'Holy Spirit, am I not happy with my body?'* Without realizing, many of us may be angry or even hate our bodies. If yes, then we can say sorry and give our anger or negative emotions to Jesus. For example, I may not like the way my body looks, or be fed-up with the chronic pain, excess acid in the stomach or chronic headaches or some other ongoing problem. If this is the case, then we can break our word-curses in Jesus' name and take authority over the area of pain or malfunction, and command it to be healed and restored, in Jesus' name. Our body responds to what we say and how we treat it. Saying sorry to our bodies is another way of forgiving self.

Body pain or fatigue, may be the result of locked in trauma, self-hate, physical overuse, emotional stress, or word-curses. The people I have met who have had the symptoms of chronic fatigue syndrome or chronic myalgia, have usually had ongoing stress, anxiety or emotional pain, which has built up in their bodies causing their bodies to feel pain or exhaustion.

The words we speak over ourselves or others are powerful. Jesus demonstrated this when He cursed the fig tree and it instantly died. There is power in what we say, for there is life and death in the tongue (Proverbs 18:21). The tongue can corrupt the whole person when it carries poison (James 3:5-12). Jesus even said we will be accountable on the Day of Judgement for every careless word we have spoken (Matthew 12:36). So we are to pay attention to the words we speak concerning ourselves and others.

Also, we don't have to agree or accept the negative words spoken by others, especially friends, relatives, enemies or even doctors. Instead, we can reject these negative words and ask God, *'God, what do You think or say concerning this?'* God's thoughts are always different to mans.

Since doctors have limited knowledge, they may sometimes get the facts wrong, or their words may sometimes sound doom and gloom. However, we have a Great Physician who knows everything and has unlimited power. Nothing is impossible or too difficult for Him. He knows the diagnosis, underlying cause and treatment required. We simply are to turn to Him for healing and have faith in what He says, especially when we have been given a poor prognosis or negative news about our health. We can reject the negative comments and possible 'curses' made by doctors or others (such as, 'you will never be able to', 'you won't or can't,' or 'you probably have so long left to live'), and replace them with what the Lord says about us. The Lord's words carry life and truth, for Jesus is the Way, the Truth and the Life (John 14:6).

Brain Studies

Brain studies have revealed how the *emotions* play a significant role in the structure and rewiring of the pathways in the brain. Our emotions cause certain parts of the brain to produce specific hormones. Certain parts of the brain, known as the hypothalamus, amygdala and hippocampus, respond to our emotions of fear, anxiety, stress, anger or joy. For example, whenever I am feeling stressed, anxious or fearful about something, my amygdala (emotion centre) will send nerve signals to my hippocampus and hypothalamus. My hypothalamus responds by releasing specific hormones that stimulate certain organs in my body, such as the adrenal glands. The adrenals then produce specific hormones that stimulate the heart and blood vessels. This causes the heart rate and blood pressure to increase, and this increases the blood flow to the muscles. So in effect, our emotions send signals to specific parts of the brain which release hormones. These hormones cause the body to act in response to our stress or fear.

Living cells respond to our thoughts and words. There is a relatively new concept in medical science known as *neuroplasticity*. Neuroplasticity is the ability for the brain to strengthen or weaken its nerve connections and form new nerves in response to our thought patterns. It's the ability of new wires and nerve connections to be formed in the brain as a result of both internal and external stimulations. Dr Caroline Leaf, a neuropsychologist, has studied the effects of 'toxic thoughts' on our bodies and believes 87-95% of mental and physical illnesses are a direct result of toxic thoughts. Toxic thoughts are negative, pessimistic, critical, or harmful thoughts. Hence, our thoughts and words have a powerful influence on our physical and mental wellbeing.[2]

Likewise, Jeffrey Barsch, an educational psychologist, has developed ways to pray for the brain[3] with children who struggle in education. The Lord revealed to him through a dream, how the power of negative words can pollute areas in the brain and compromise the level of brain function and intellect. A small group of children who had Attention Deficit Disorder (ADD) were found to have something in common. They had been rejected or not wanted whilst in the womb either by the mother, father or grandparents. Apparently, the children no longer had ADD to the same extent once this rejection was addressed.

When negative words are exchanged for God's words of truth and blessings, then our brain function and intellect may significantly improve. This is because neurons (or nerve cells) and dendrites respond to the words we think and speak, whether the words are blessings or curses.

Studies have shown it usually takes at least four weeks, if not more, for a new thought (or belief) to form a new neurone or pathway in the brain. This is the process known as 'rewiring', where old toxic or negative thoughts are replaced or rewired with positive and Godly thoughts. This is why it is important to declare any truths we receive from the Spirit for at least four weeks, until it has become ingrained in our mind and forms a new pathway in our belief system. Transformation is an ongoing process that is achieved by the renewing or rewiring of our minds (Romans 12:2).

Blessing the Body

Sometimes when I am out walking or doing something, I may feel a pain or discomfort in an area of my body. In most cases when I take authority over the symptoms and command them to leave followed by blessing that part of my body, the symptoms usually go within minutes or the next hour or so. However, in some cases the symptoms may persist or take much longer to go and require medical or spiritual attention. There was a time when I felt numbness down my right arm for no apparent reason and I instantly rebuked it and commanded it to leave. Within seconds the numbness went and my arm felt normal again.

Below are some examples of how to bless the various parts of our body. Certain areas of our body that are not functioning so well may require more prayer compared to others, so we can pray more appropriately where needed. For example, if I happen to have an organ, like my bowel, which isn't functioning properly or has problems, then instead of being negative by saying, *'I'm constantly having problems with my bowel....I suffer with indigestion...I have terrible pain from acid reflux...my bowels can't function normally...,'* I can replace these words with blessings such as, *'Thank you God for my bowel. I am sorry if I have put my bowel under stress, and repent of all the word curses I may have spoken. I command my acid levels to be normal in Jesus' name. I come against any pain or discomfort and command my bowel to function normally, in Jesus' name. I bless my bowel with the Shalom of the Lord, to function normally and be at rest.'*

I have met Christians who have asked me to pray for various parts of their body to be healed. Instead, I get them to minister to themselves. First, we ask the Holy Spirit to highlight if there is anything they may need to repent of or say sorry for doing that may have inflicted the symptoms. Or perhaps there is someone to forgive, or they are to forgive themselves. Next, they can take authority against the pain or body issue and command it to go. If the problem has been generational, then I encourage them to forgive their parents, grandparents and forefathers, in their mother's or father's blood line. Then they can bless that part of their body to function normally and declare the 'shalom' or peace of the Lord upon it.

One thing to note is there is not much point in praying for your body if you don't believe in the power of your words or the spiritual authority you carry. It only works if you speak with faith and authority. Faith and authority release healing. Don't give up if nothing happens immediately. Keep declaring words of life and health, and your body cells respond to your faith and authority. Sometimes, it takes time for our body to realign back to normal, just like a neglected plant in a garden takes time to grow back through regular watering. Jesus said: *'If you have faith as small as a mustard seed, you can say to this mulberry tree, 'Be uprooted and planted in the sea' and it will obey you'* (Luke 17:6). Jesus was referring to speaking to something living that doesn't even have a brain. If we can say this to a tree, how much more can we command our bodies with the power of our words, when spoken with faith?

Likewise, we should take care of our bodies by eating healthily and doing regular exercise. There is not much point in blessing only to contaminate with smoking, excess alcohol or an unhealthy diet.

Spirit of Gluttony

Many people comfort eat when they feel down, alone, or rejected. Sadly, the comfort gained from eating is short lived. However, excessive eating may lead to being overweight, and this affects our mental and physical wellbeing. Some struggle with self-control when it comes to eating and this is probably because they have come under a *spirit of gluttony.*

There was a woman who was overweight and admitted that she 'loved' her food and comfort ate most of the time. She would easily consume a whole bar of chocolate and eat a piece or two of cake most days. She asked for prayer to help overcome her eating habit. It transpired that the main root was self-hate, and the Holy Spirit revealed to her spirit how she had come under a spirit of gluttony. After she received inner healing for her self-hate, she was able to renounce the spirit of gluttony. Subsequently, she was able to resist the temptation to eat a whole chocolate bar, and started to lose some weight.

Declare Health and Life over our Body

Here are some general points for blessing the body. However, in certain cases, further ministry may be required to deal with any underlying or deep rooted issues.

If there is pain, swelling, disease or inflammation, we can start by commanding it to go in Jesus' name. Or if you know the cause, such as excess acid in stomach, or constriction of airways, or inflamed joints, or high blood pressure etc, then speak to this part and declare the opposite. So, you can tell your acid levels to reduce to normal; airways to relax; lubrication to flow in the joints; blood pressure to return to normal, and so on. Where an organ requires healing, then command the organ to be healed and return to optimum function in Jesus' Name. After this, we can cleanse the area with the blood of Jesus and declare by His wounds we are healed (Isaiah 53:5). We can finish by praying the peace of God to rest on our body (instead of stress, fear, angst...) and thank God for healing our body.

There was a lady who was feeling tired and dizzy as a result of being anaemic, and asked for prayer. I got her to break off any word-curse spoken over her health and then to take authority over her bone marrow, commanding the red blood cells to produce healthy levels. She took authority over her symptoms and blessed her body with the peace of God. When I saw her the next week at church, she said her symptoms went the next day and she felt much better.

There was a man in a meeting who had a chronic dry cough, but I noticed he only coughed when someone else was praying. I sensed his cough may have a spiritual root, so I invited him to put his hand over his throat and command the cough to leave in Jesus' name. As he did, he felt something leave him and the cough stopped. Following this, I got him to bless his throat.

There was a retired lady who had been diagnosed with peripheral neuropathy. There was no treatment available for the ongoing pain she felt in her feet and lower legs. Sometimes her feet felt numb, and other times they tingled or became painful and kept her awake at night. After a strenuous day in the garden, the pain increased and became unbearable. Then she decided to speak to her peripheral nerves and feet. She gently yet firmly told her feet and peripheral nerves how she was sorry if she had done too much in the garden. Then she took authority over the pain and commanded it to stop. She released the peace of God on her feet. The pain significantly reduced and her sleeping improved.

Sometimes, we may have to deal with the root behind the issue. For example, there can be different reasons why women may develop breast lumps or breast cancer. A common underlying root is having an issue with another woman. Many have had issues with their grandmother, mother, aunt, sister or female colleagues. Once these female relationships are addressed and curses broken, healing may flow. Having a problem with another woman may affect the feminine organs, especially the breasts. Hence, it is good for women to be at peace with other female relationships, and no longer hold on to grudges, hurts, bitterness or resentment.

Here are some examples of how to pray for different parts of the body. You can do it when out walking, during exercise, having a shower, when you get up in the morning, or however you choose.

BRAIN: *'Lord Jesus, I thank You for my brain. I undo the negative words I have spoken or heard others say, and choose to bless my intellect,* my short and long-term memory and my emotions. May they function to their optimum capacity. I bless my synapses (connections between nerves), my dendrites and neurones to interact with each other and form new pathways. I bless my brain lobes and all that's in my brain stem. I bless my chemicals and hormones to be at healthy levels, including normal glucose and oxygen. I bless my eyes, ears and senses to function to their optimum capacity, both in the natural and supernatural. Lord, open my eyes to see you more, my ears to hear You more and increase my levels of discernment. I ask for Your Spirit of Wisdom, Revelation, Knowledge, Counsel and Might and Fear of the Lord to instruct and guide me. Sanctify my mind and imagination with Your blood, so I may think and see from Your perspective and in Your Spirit. I bless my emotion centre to be at rest and overflow with the joy of the Lord. I surrender any fears or anxious thoughts to You, and welcome Your peace in my mind and heart. I bless my brain to have the supernatural ability to understand and remember the word of God. Lord, filter out any ungodly thoughts and cleanse my brain from any demonic influences that have prevented me from hearing, seeing and feeling your Presence. Lord, protect what I hear, see and think from now on, in Jesus' name.

NERVES & SPINAL CORD: *'I bless my spinal cord and peripheral nerves in my arms and legs to function with normal sensation of touch, pain, heat, vibration and sense of position. I pray protection on the nerve sheaths (coverings) and for healing where there has been any damage. I command my spinal cord to come into alignment and bless the vertebral discs with optimum function. I forgive myself if I have overdone it. I release any trapped nerves from pressure, and speak freedom and healing in Jesus' Name.*

HEART & BLOOD: *'Thank you Lord for my heart. I bless each chamber, valve and all blood vessels to have normal function. Lord, cleanse and remove any debris or blockage in my vessels where needed. I bless my electrical wiring and for my heart to beat normally and in rhythm with Your heart beat. I bless my blood pressure to be normal. I command my blood pressure to come down (or go up) to normal range in Jesus' name! Also, I command my cholesterol levels to come down to healthy levels. I cleanse my blood with the sanctifying work of Your blood, and bless it to flow smoothly through my vessels. May Your blood cleanse every cell in my body. I bless my heart to be strong, both physically and emotionally. Jesus, protect it with Your love and the covering of Your blood.*

LUNGS: *'Thank you Lord for my lungs. I command any spasms or inflammation in my airways to go in Jesus' name! I command any blockages to unblock in Jesus' Name and for my airways to relax and rest with the peace of the Lord. I breathe in the Spirit of God and exhale any impurities. I breathe in Your Spirit of peace and exhale any stress or angst (do this more than once if needed).*

Lord, protect my nose, mouth and airways from any infection by the sanctifying work of Your blood. I pray blessings on my lungs and airways to have maximum function.

BONES & JOINTS: *'Forgive me, if I have spoken negatively about anyone or to anyone. I am sorry and forgive them for what they have done or said that has hurt me. And I forgive myself where needed. Lord, forgive me for any anger or bitterness. I no longer want to hold on to it. I give it to You. Cleanse my bones and joints from all toxins, with Your blood. Thank you for my bones. I bless them to be strong and resilient. I command my blood cells (my red blood cells, white blood cells and platelets) to optimum production and function. I bless my joints to full range of movement and to be lubricated by the oil of the Spirit. I bless all tendons and ligaments to be strong. I bless all joints to move in the various positions, especially the positions for praise and worship.*

BACK & MUSCLES: *'I bless my muscles with full power and strength. I bind any spasm and command pain or inflammation to go in Jesus' Name. I speak peace and rest over all my muscles and full flexibility as needed (lay your hands on any muscles requiring healing). I bless my discs with full resilience and elasticity and normal alignment in my back. May my body, soul and spirit be in alignment with Your will. And where I have overused or strained any muscle, I am sorry for doing this, and I bless the fibres to function normally, and declare peace and rest to you.*

IMMUNE SYSTEM: *'I bless my immune system to optimum function. I bless my lymph glands, spleen and bone marrow, to produce the correct immune-globulins (anti-bodies) where needed. I speak peace and unity over my immune system and bless you to protect my body against sickness and disease. Forgive me if I have put you under stress. Lord, cleanse my immune system from anything not of You (infection, cancer...). Purify it with Your blood. And I bless my immune system to function under the divine protection of the Lord.*

GUT: *'Lord thank you for my gut. I forgive myself if I have put my gut under any stress or eaten anything I shouldn't have. I renounce any spirit of gluttony. I bless my gut to function normally and move in the right direction. I speak peace throughout my gut, from my mouth to my bottom. I command acid levels to return to normal levels, and peace over my bowel motions. I command my gut flora to be healthy. Also, I bless my pancreas to produce normal insulin and command my sugar levels to be normal. I bless my whole digestive system with the peace of the Lord.*

LIVER: *'I bless my liver to have normal function as it cleanses and detoxifies the substances in my body. Lord, cleanse and restore any diseased area with the power of Your blood. Forgive me if I have abused my liver with alcohol or drugs. I am sorry and I renounce any spirit of addiction. I speak life and health over my liver in Jesus' name.*

SKIN & HAIR: *'I bless my skin and command any cancerous cell or infective cell to shrink and die in Jesus' Name. Lord, cleanse my skin with Your blood and protect it from any harm. I bless my hair roots to grow healthy strands of hair as in my youth.*

TEETH & GUMS: *'I bless my teeth to be strengthened with enamel. I command any infection or decay to go in Jesus' Name. Forgive me for abusing or causing harm in any way. Teeth and gums be strong and healthy as in my youth.*

HANDS & FEET: *'I bless my hands and wrists to do all I need to do and my feet to take me where I need to go. Forgive me for any repetitive injury or strain on my joints. I speak peace and blessing over every joint and muscle. I command fasciitis and swelling (or anything else) to go in Jesus name. I bless the arches in my feet, and joints in my hand.*

KIDNEYS & ADRENALS: *'I bless my kidneys to filter and maintain correct water and electrolyte levels in my body. I bless my adrenals to produce healthy levels of steroids, adrenaline and other hormones as needed, especially during moments of stress. I bless you to have optimum function. I am sorry for allowing prolonged periods of stress, fear or anxiety. Forgive me. I speak peace and rest over my adrenals, and bless you in the name of Jesus.*

SEXUAL ORGANS:
For women: *'I bless my feminine organs to function normally and command my hormones to come to normal levels. I command hot flushes to stop and bless my thermoregulatory centre to be healthy. Lord cleanse and purify my organs with Your blood, so I may be pure and holy unto You. I bless my femininity as a mother, wife, sister, daughter and bride of Christ. (Repent of any sexual sin, and forgive the women who have hurt you).*

For men: *'I bless my genitalia to normal function and command my hormones to normal levels. I bless my masculinity as a father, brother, husband, son and follower of Christ. Lord cleanse and purify me with Your blood, so I may be pure and holy unto You (repent of sexual sins or impure thoughts where needed).*

These prayers can be modified and altered as needed. They are simply a guide to pray blessings and take authority over the cells and organs in our body. In some cases, blessing the body may not be enough and further ministry may be required to address the deeper issues in the heart. However, I believe blessing the body can be a valuable tool for our daily health and wellbeing.

ENDNOTES:

[1] Capps, Charles; *God's Creative Power for Healing*; (*Capps Publishing, 1991*)
[2] Dr Leaf, Caroline: *Who switched off my brain? Controlling toxic thoughts and emotions*; (*IBD, 2008*)
[3] Barsch, Jeffrey; *Praying for the Brain; Educational Sozo* (*Beneath His Wings Publishing Company, 2013*)

11

Breaking Soul-Ties

Do you not know that he who unites himself with a prostitute is one with her in body?

1 Corinthians 6:16

A soul-tie is formed when we connect or tie our soul to *people, places* or *things*. It is an invisible spiritual or emotional bond. Soul-ties may be godly or ungodly.

Soul-Ties with People

Godly Soul-ties

Godly soul-ties develop in healthy relationships and are formed in relationships where there is unconditional love. This type of relationship leads to freedom and wholeness in body, soul and spirit. Paul outlines a healthy marriage: *'Wives, submit to your husband as to the Lord....Husbands, love your wives, just as Christ loved the church and gave Himself up for her, to make her holy...'* (Ephesians 5:22-32).

David had a godly relationship with Jonathan, where they became one in spirit: *'Jonathan became one in sprit with David and he loved him as himself,'* (1 Samuel 18:1). This relationship was based on unconditional, sacrificial, brotherly love, where they both cared more for the other than themselves.

Godly soul-ties are also made when we make a vow or covenant with God, by choosing to follow Him. We are 'bonded' to God in a pure, loving way as we choose to serve Him. God wants us to be first and foremost bonded to Him, and then to each other. Hence, the first command is to love the Lord our God with all our heart, mind, soul and strength, and the second command is to love our neighbour *as ourselves.*

Ungodly Soul-ties
Ungodly soul-ties come about as a result of unhealthy relationships where a person may feel 'pulled' or yoked to someone. These may be sexual or non-sexual relationships, and can taint our relationship with God and with others.

Most of us will have developed an ungodly soul-tie from one or more relationships in our lifetime. These are relationships that exhibit ungodly characteristics such as conditional love, fear or control, reverse parenting (where the child looks after the parent), a victim mindset, fear of man (or the need to please man), emotional manipulation, idolatry or worshipping someone, or any form of abuse.

A sexual relationship with someone outside of marriage produces an ungodly sexual soul-tie even if it just happens once. Likewise, ungodly soul-ties may occur in an abusive marriage. Ungodly soul-ties can occur in any relationship, such as with parents, siblings, teachers, pastors, therapists, church members, bosses and staff, and the list goes on. Any controlling or manipulative relationship bears unhealthy soul-ties. Ungodly soul-ties can affect the body, soul and spirit, as a result of emotional stress and spiritual bondage.

I met an old woman in Mozambique who was considered to be an elder in her tribe. For years she had been involved in an ungodly sexual relationship with a witchdoctor and desperately wanted to break free from him. She had been looking for some other 'power' that could set her free. She presented with body pain in her hip and leg and an infected red eye. After I told her about Jesus, the Son of God, she gladly welcomed Him into her heart. I led her in prayer as she broke her soul-ties with the witchdoctor. Her pain immediately left her hip and leg, and her eye no longer felt inflamed. She had encountered the love and healing power of Jesus as she broke free from the witchdoctor and now became bonded to Jesus. As a result, she wanted to tell others in her village about her new friend Jesus.

There was a lady who had been involved in many sexual relationships that had prevented her bonding with her husband. She said she still felt 'tied' to these previous relationships. So she repented and then broke the soul-ties with each of her past sexual partners. After this, she was able to spiritually connect with her husband and enjoy intimacy with him.

All unhealthy soul-ties are to be broken. As mentioned, we can have an unhealthy soul tie with anyone. Also, soul-ties may be linked to an ungodly spirit, depending on the spirit(s) the other person may carry. It is possible to have a healthy relationship with someone, like your parents, friends and spouse, but have unhealthy soul-ties where there are flaws in the relationship. The unhealthy soul-ties can be broken and the healthy ones maintained. For example, I may have a good relationship with someone but there is an element of control where the person keeps telling me what to do or tries to manipulate me into doing things for them. Where there is an unhealthy soul-tie of control and manipulation, I can break this and not allow myself to be influenced by it, yet remain in the relationship. This requires learning to say 'no' instead of being a people pleaser (Galatians 1:10). Many 'people pleasers' carry the 'fear of man'. They want to please for they fear the consequences if they don't, or fear possible rejection. These issues may be addressed by developing healthy boundaries in our relationships.[1]

Once soul-ties have been broken, people may feel they have gained a part of themselves back. They feel free and no longer pulled or tugged by the other person's spirit or emotions, since they no longer feel afraid or obliged to do what the other person wants. Some have experienced purity being restored after sexual soul-ties were broken.

When I was living in South Sudan, I had the opportunity to minister to a group of youth, aged from sixteen to thirty. When I asked the Lord what to do, He said to speak on soul-ties. I sensed most, if not all, had been involved in sexual relationships. So instead of embarrassing anyone, I led them all through repentance and the breaking of soul-ties. Afterwards, I spoke to a young man and asked what he thought of the session. He smiled and said he had gained something back which was valuable to him and God.

There was a lady who left her husband when she realized he was abusive and controlling. She felt so imprisoned by this relationship that she ended up filing for a divorce. After a teaching on *Soul-Ties,* this lady forgave her ex-husband for all he did to her and broke the ungodly soul-tie. As she did this, she let out a loud noise. She later commented that once the soul-tie was broken she felt she had regained her freedom.

Paul said we are to be careful who we become joined to: '*Do you not know that he who unites himself with a prostitute is one with her body? But he who unites himself with the Lord is one with Him in Spirit*' (1 Corinthians 6:15-17).

One lady struggled to say the words to forgive her father because he had controlled her voice throughout childhood. I realised we had to break the controlling soul-tie with her father in order for her to regain self-control over her voice. As she broke the soul-tie, she gave back to her father what was his and took back what had been taken from her, including her freedom to speak and self-control over her voice. Instantly, she was able to speak the words of forgiveness towards her father.

Sometimes people may struggle to move on in life after a spouse, relative or close friend has died because they are holding on to the person as if the dead person is still alive. In such cases, I suggest breaking the soul-ties with the deceased person as they hand the person to Jesus. This can release freedom from grief as they let go of the past. Their memories for the deceased will still remain but they are now free to start living again.

Soul-Ties with Places

Some people may find it hard to separate themselves from a place or home. Without realising, they may have made a vow '*I will never leave here*' or '*I always want to live/work here*'. It is important to let go of our home, job or place where there has been any emotional or spiritual attachment, so we can be free to move on to where God wants us to be. One of the important things I learnt whilst on the mission field was to release myself from any emotional or spiritual connections to each mission base. I would give the base and people back to God, releasing myself from any responsibility, and in my own words say goodbye and pray a blessing over the people. After this, my spirit would feel free to go where the Lord was leading me next.

A fellow missionary had to urgently return to the UK and was unable to say goodbye to the people or base. As a result, she felt her flesh was in the UK, but her spirit and heart were still at the base in Africa. So she returned to the base, to say goodbye. When she came back to the UK, she felt her whole self had returned and could focus whole heartedly on her new job.

When I decided to rent out my home before going to Africa, the Lord convicted me of being too emotionally attached, and I had to surrender my home to Him. I shed some tears as I let it go, and He said that though I owned it on paper, it now belonged to Him. This released me from the emotional soul-tie I had formed with my home and I now felt fine about renting it out to others.

A retired woman had many times said that she never wanted to leave her area because she had lived there for many years. However, after her husband died, she wanted to move closer to where her daughter lived but something was holding her back. The Lord convicted her of having a soul-tie with her area. Once she broke the soul-tie, she was free to move to a new area.

Soul-Ties with Things

Sometimes, people may struggle to give up something because it means too much or they can't live without it. Again, this may be something to surrender to God in order to be set free from any ungodly yoke. For example, a person may be attached to an expensive or sentimental possession, or to a pet. If we feel a strong connection to something, then it is good and liberating to simply let go, by giving it over to God. This doesn't necessarily mean we have to get rid of it, but rather we will no longer feel tied to it.

In the case of addictions, a person may have a soul-tie with the thing they are addicted to and the healing includes breaking the soul-tie with the addictive substance or activity.

How to Break Soul-Ties

This is relatively simple as we bring each place or thing to Jesus and simply hand it over to Him. In the case of relational soul-ties, we can express any wrong doing on our part and then proceed to forgive the other people. It is powerful when we imagine the individual(s) standing in front, as we express our words of hurt and forgiveness to them.

The soul-tie can be broken as we command any spirit attached to the relationship to return to where it came from, in Jesus' name. This should be said with authority by commanding any ungodly spirit (such as the spirit of control, manipulation, abuse, rape, witchcraft, intimidation, violation and so on), to leave in Jesus' name. Some find it helpful to imagine holding a sword (or the sword of the Spirit) as they cut the soul-tie(s).

Next, we can claim back anything that the other person has taken or stolen. This may be a part of our emotions, thoughts, identity or spirit. For example, it may be our self-respect, dignity, self-confidence, self-control, purity, voice, identity and so on. We can pray something like this to break a sexual or ungodly soul-tie:

'In the name of Jesus, I break all ungodly soul-ties with ……(name the person). I give back everything that is theirs and take back everything I gave away including….(my free will, self-control, body, voice/freedom to speak, purity, identity (including masculinity or femininity) etc'. Finally, we ask the Lord to cleanse us with His blood.

In some cases, it may be we are the ones who have been controlling, manipulative or abusive in our relationship towards others and this means we are to repent as we release each person back to Jesus. There was a man who heard my teaching on soul-ties and when it came to asking the Holy Spirit about unhealthy soul-ties with people, he was instantly convicted of his relationship with his daughter who was at university. He realised that she was still attached to his apron strings and he had to let go of control over his child's life. There was a relief as the father broke the unhealthy soul-tie and then released his child to Jesus, giving his child the freedom to make her own decisions.

Sometimes, we may have to do this more than once with the same person if an unhealthy soul-tie forms again. It is liberating when soul-ties are broken from places, things, or ungodly relationships and is easy to do.

END NOTES

[1] Dr Cloud & Dr Townsend: *Boundaries (Zondervan, 2017)*

12

Overcoming Sexual Issues

*We have one who has been tempted in every way,
just as we are – yet was without sin*

Hebrews 4:15

One of the lusts of the flesh may disguise as a false pleasure or comfort, or a way to escape from the stresses of life. It is like a poisonous weed that is looking for an entrance into our spiritual garden (or inner being). The moment it's in the ground, it will start to take root unless we acknowledge it as sin and uproot it. However, if we choose to allow it in, then the deeper the roots will grow and spread, as they try to infiltrate the rest of our spiritual garden. The enemy is prowling around as a wolf in lamb's clothing, and his mission is to steal, kill and destroy, by whatever means he can. One of his ways is to lure man's soul through enticing him or her into sexual sin and bondage.

Nowadays, people are being lured into pornography or unhealthy sexual relationships, through social media, peer pressure and access to the internet. Sexual issues are rarely discussed in the church, but undoubtedly affect our relationship with God and each other.

Many who struggle with sexual issues may have been abused, traumatized or neglected during their earlier years in childhood. Sexual issues may carry a sense of shame, blame, self-hate or pain. Here are some useful tools to help lead a person to healing and freedom.

What is the Access Point?
One of the important things, as with all issues, is to find the access point or root to the symptoms. Where or when did it begin? This may or may not be known, and depends if the person has blocked out any painful memories from childhood. In some cases, it may be the result of peer pressure at school or family issues at home. As we ask the Holy Spirit to reveal when it took root, the person may be reminded of a memory of an event that occurred.

Some may not want to recall the memories due to a sense of fear, blame, guilt, or shame. Hence, it is important the person feels safe and a sense of God's Presence during the ministry session. This is why it is good to welcome the Presence of God into the session if this hasn't already been done at the beginning.

Dealing with Unclean Spirits
Usually there are unclean spirits attached to sexual sin. For example, a person who is struggling with sexual sin may be affected by one or more of the following unclean spirits: *lust, perversion, seduction, promiscuity, fornication, rape, incest, molestation, pornography, ungodly sexual spirits, sexual gratification and defilement.* Each of these unclean spirits can be confessed and renounced where applicable.

There was a lady who asked for prayer after I taught on soul-ties. She openly confessed to having sexual relationships as well as lust and being involved in pornography. She wanted to have a pure heart and rededicate her life completely to Jesus, so she repented and renounced the unclean spirits, and received cleansing for her spirit, soul and body with the blood of Jesus. She felt something leave as purity returned to her heart.

Many times Jesus ministered to people who were prostitutes or had committed adultery. In one case, He forgave a woman who was about to be stoned and lovingly told her to sin no more (John 8:1-11).

A person may confess their sin and renounce the unclean spirits, but the root may still need to be addressed. Dealing with the root is an important step in healing and freedom. Equally, it is important to keep the door to sin closed by choosing not to entertain it again. Paul said: *'Do not let the sun go down while you are still angry, and do not give the devil a foot-hold'* (Ephesians 4:27). Hence, we are to resist the spirit of lust, sexual gratification and so on, especially when it knocks on the door of our minds and hearts. And if we do entertain it by opening the door in our heart, then we are to recognise this and kick it out by commanding the spirit(s) to leave in Jesus' Name, and cleansing our hearts and minds with the sanctifying blood of Jesus.

Generational Sin

People may have inherited sexual issues from their parents or ancestors. Sexual sins are commonly passed down the bloodline especially when the same issue is seen to repeat itself. Some may have sexual issues due to lack of love or poor parenting. The parents may have been unloved by their parents and this lack of love may be passed down the blood line. Repentance and forgiveness, along with cleansing by the blood of Jesus, can prevent the sin from being passed to the next generations.

A lady realised how shame had been past down her mother's blood-line, from her grandmother to her mum to herself but didn't know why. The Holy Spirit highlighted the root cause was sexual abuse, so we ministered healing in this area of her heart and she was freed from all shame. (For more on freedom from sexual abuse read Chapter 9 in *Divine Heart Surgery*).

Wounded Emotions

Most sexual issues are usually linked to wounded emotions, such as anger, rejection, abandonment, not good enough, self-hate or hatred to others, shame and guilt. Each of these emotions may be attached to an ungodly spirit. As the person recognizes their wounded emotions, they can give each emotion to Jesus.

If a person is struggling to forgive others or themselves, then we can ask Jesus for His amazing grace to help them forgive. With this same grace, Jesus was able to forgive those who verbally and physically abused Him as He hung on the cross. Remember, forgiveness powerfully releases us from bondage, when we forgive from our heart.

Jesus can give us something in exchange for our negative or wounded emotions. It may be a sense of feeling loved, pure and accepted by Him. Whatever it is, He will minister to the heart and emotional needs of each person who wants to be cleansed and set free.

Breaking Sexual Soul-Ties
Where a person has been involved in sexual relationships or sexual abuse, then the sexual soul-ties are to be broken. Freedom is received as they take back what is theirs, including their purity, dignity, freedom to speak, free will, etc (See previous chapter for more details).

Cleansing the Body, Soul & Spirit
Once the areas that require repentance and forgiveness are addressed, the person can receive cleansing with the powerful blood of Jesus. His blood is like supernatural bleach, removing all unclean spirits and defilement. I usually allow a few minutes for the person to receive cleansing in their body, soul and spirit.

Many Israelites received cleansing and healing as they entered certain pools, for example the pool called Bethesda in Jerusalem (see John 5). An amazing way to receive inner cleansing is to imagine oneself in sanctified water, such as, standing under a divine waterfall, or entering a sanctified pool, or soaking in the ocean of His Presence, or the river of Life. As the person imagines themselves in the sanctified water, I pray cleansing and healing through the blood of Jesus, as the water washes away the ungodly spirits attached to their negative emotions. The cleansing process only takes a few minutes until the person feels cleansed and pure inside. Many want to remain in the water for it feels great.

During this process we can pray for the cleansing of the memory cells in the mind, emotion, body and spirit.

Encountering Jesus
After the cleansing procedure, I usually invite the person to encounter Jesus. Most find this relatively easy to do, hence, I

invite the person to welcome Jesus, and ask Him what He would like to say or perhaps give to them. He loves to give us new things in exchange for our filthy rags. We can ask Jesus how does He see them? This is a significant part of the healing for it connects the person's heart to Jesus. Some have testified to Jesus holding out His hand to them and smiling, or receiving rings of betrothal, or spiritual swords. Women may see themselves wearing a white dress or new garment bearing spiritual significance. The exchange of contaminated clothes for something new is powerful and helps reconcile the person's heart back to Jesus.

We read something similar in Zechariah, where Joshua the high priest was standing with filthy clothes before the Lord. As his filthy clothes were taken off, the Lord removed his sin and in exchange gave him rich garments to wear. After this, a turban was put on his head (Zechariah 3:1-7). The turban is a covering for the head and can represent the renewing of our mind with the mind of Christ.

I saw a lady who for years had suppressed her feelings of rejection, failure and defilement. There were three men in her life that she had had a sexual relationship with, and each had let her down in one way or another. As we dealt with each relationship, she repented of her wrong doings and forgave them for what they did. Next, I led her to break the soul-ties with each relationship as she imagined each of the men standing in front of her. After this, I got her to imagine herself walking in a sanctified pool and to receive cleansing of her whole being. She felt completely cleansed and pure as she got out of the water. Next, she was able to reconnect her heart to Jesus as she looked into His eyes of love. She said her past relationships had tainted her relationship with Jesus and only now could she see Him through the eyes of love. Her heart had been re-united to Jesus after she felt cleansed, loved and accepted once again. She simply glowed and kept smiling as if something amazing had happened in her heart and spirit.

Premarital Sex & Adultery

God created sex for the relationship between a husband and wife. Sex outside of marriage carries health issues, including the risk of unwanted pregnancies and abortions, sexually transmitted diseases, and cervical cancer. A soul-tie is formed during sexual intercourse, even if it's just a once off. *'Do you not know that he who unites himself to a prostitute is one with her in body? For it is said, "The two will become one flesh". But he who unites himself with the Lord, is one with Him in spirit,'* (1 Corinthians 6:16-17).

When a sexual relationship doesn't lead to marriage, the person may feel to some extent defiled or worthless since they have given an important part of themselves to someone. Likewise, if a person has been abused or raped, they may feel their virginity has been violated. As a person loses their purity and virginity it will affect their sense of self-worth and dignity. The beautiful thing is as we ask Jesus to cleanse us from all sexual defilement, our sense of self-worth and purity is restored.

I knew a woman who had a sexual relationship with her first boyfriend. She was falsely misled into believing that he loved her, until he finished the relationship for someone else. She happened to be in another relationship when she personally had an encounter with Jesus, and instantly knew this boyfriend was not right. Jesus not only came into her heart, but He healed and restored her inner being. After her encounter with Jesus, she testified to feeling pure inside, as if her virginity was restored.

Medical research has shown that a virus named *Human Papilloma Virus* (HPV) is responsible for most cervical cancers in sexually active women. Sadly, there are young women who are dying as a result of acquiring HPV through pre-marital sexual relationships. A vaccine has been developed to prevent HPV in teenage girls, though I believe the best prevention is to abstain from sex until marriage. If someone truly loves another person, then they will keep themselves pure until the wedding day. True love never forces another person to have sex, but honours the person and respects their body. Sex outside of marriage may lead to other sexually transmitted diseases (STD). Though the Lord can heal all STD's, He wants our hearts to engage in a pure relationship with Him. Jesus said: *'Blessed are the pure in heart, for they will see God'* (Matthew 5:8).

Jesus said we commit adultery whenever we look at someone with lustful eyes: *'I tell you that anyone who looks at a woman lustfully has already committed adultery with her in his heart. If your right eye causes you to sin, gouge it out and throw it away. It is better for you to lose one part of your body that for your whole body to be thrown in hell,'* (Matthew 5:27-30). The Lord wants to cleanse and heal His children from having lustful eyes and perverse thoughts. As we present each case to Jesus, we can receive His forgiveness and cleansing, through the power of His blood. Guilt, shame, lust and perverse thoughts can be removed, soul-ties can be broken, and purity can be restored, when we turn our hearts to Him.

Pornography

In the last few years, Christians have openly asked me for ministry concerning their involvement with pornography. Pornography is a huge area to be addressed in the body of Christ. It is preventing people from drawing closer to God or stepping into their calling and ministry.

Many Spirit-filled believers, even well known leaders, may be struggling in this area. There are different reasons behind such cravings. Some say it is to escape from the stress of work or their nagging spouse. Others may be struggling with their spiritual identity, because of issues with their father. However, sometimes it may be an attack from demonic forces to affect a person's ministry. Whenever a sexual spirit is discerned in the body of Christ, we can ask the Holy Spirit if this is an internal issue or external attack. Internal issues require inner healing for the individual, whereas external attacks require spiritual covering and intercession. One of the enemy's weapons in these End-Times is to attack the body of Christ with the spirit of lust, seduction and pornography (read Revelation 17).

I was stunned with tears in my eyes when I heard a well known man of God openly confess to his involvement with pornography. One day when he was feeling vulnerable and tired, a sexual picture popped up on his computer. He clicked the picture and became drawn to pornography. After he bravely confessed this at a conference, another leader also openly confessed to the same sin. These were men of God who had been doing major battles on the front line, and the enemy had sent hordes of sexual demons to attack and pull them down. My tears were of sorrow and intercession as I prayed for these men. I saw the importance of covering one another in prayer, and to deal immediately with the sin as it arises.

The enemy is constantly polluting minds and hearts through sexual images and perverse thoughts on bill boards, posters, books, newspapers and throughout the social media. The purpose is to lure people away from God, and destroy the younger generation, as well as families or those in ministry. We are to love the people but hate the sin.

False Power & False Pleasure
Pornography provides false power, false pleasure and false comfort as it feeds the flesh or carnal nature, and quenches the spirit. I believe most cases result from soul-wounds where a person's emotional needs have not been met by their parents or spouse. When an emotional wound is triggered, the person may seek comfort or power through pornography. The flesh may respond to sexual cravings in the same way it does to an addiction. Hence, the person craves for an erotic or 'high' feeling which may make the person feel 'empowered'. As part of the freedom and healing ministry, the person is to 'dis-empower' this false power. It is liberating when they choose to declare this false power powerless and for the person to no longer want it. Also, the person can renounce any unclean spirits such as lust, perversion, and sexual fantasy etc.

John warns about feeding the lustful desires of the flesh: *'If anyone loves the world, the love of the Father is not in him. For everything in the world- the **cravings of sinful man, the lust of his eyes**, and **the boasting of what he has and does**- comes not from the Father but from the world,'* (1 John 2:16). It is deception to believe pornography is not harmful and just a bit of pleasure. It becomes harmful as this repeated behaviour develops into a habit. Toxic paths are created and wired in the brain each time a person engages in pornography, and this can form a habitual pathway.

Pornography may include prostitution, adultery (or seeing someone with lustful eyes), sex chats on the phone or internet. As the lustful thoughts become repetitive, a wiring or pathway forms in the brain which soon forms into a habit. If it isn't stopped, then it will become an addiction which feeds the flesh that is not yielded to God.

Hate the Sin

One key to being healed and set free from pornography is the person is to hate the sin more than the pleasure it gives. Many repent, but are not set free because they do not hate the sin enough. I heard a testimony from a well known teacher and Bible preacher, who kept sinning even though he repented of the sin. He asked God why he was not set free from the sin and the Lord replied, it was because he didn't hate the sin enough.

There are testimonies of people who were set free from a *spirit* of pornography and as a result no longer entertained it. However, others may have to resist the habit by daily refusing to entertain it, and choosing to turn their hearts and minds to the Lord. How desperate are we to follow Jesus and be set free from this habit? The Lord will help us as we willingly take responsibility for our thoughts and actions, and avoid all sources of temptations. This may mean setting boundaries or finding someone with whom to be accountable to. If the boundaries aren't working, then they may need to be further extended.

Ministry Session

The first question is when did the pornography begin? If the person doesn't remember, then we can ask the Holy Spirit to highlight the memory when the seed was sown. For some, it may be when they were introduced to a magazine or saw pop-up photos on their mobile phone. Once the root is addressed, the person can be led to repent of their sin and forgive where needed from the heart. If there are any sexual spirits or spirits attached to the emotions, then these can be renounced (eg spirit of lust, prostitution, promiscuity, seduction, perversion, etc). The person is to choose to hate the sin in order to dis-empower the power behind the false pleasure. I encourage the person to pray something like this: *'I renounce any spirit of pornography, spirit of lust and perversion in Jesus' Name. I disempower the power behind this craving. It is not my friend but my enemy, so I break all soul-ties with pornography in Jesus' name.'* Next, any memories of defiled images can be washed off and cleansed through the sanctifying power of the blood of Jesus. Where there may be any emotional wounds, such as rejection and abandonment, these may be addressed as the person invites Jesus into their trauma memory.

A woman came to see me to be set free from unclean thoughts and masturbation. The Lord brought back the memory of when she was a little child and found her father watching pornography on the TV. These graphic images had tainted her soul and spirit, though she had not pursued pornography herself. So as we invited Jesus into the memory, she started to cry. She repented of allowing this to happen and forgave her father. Next, she saw Jesus hold her hand and lead her out of the room. As she kept her eyes on Him, the defiled images faded away. She repented of masturbation and other sexual desires that had arisen as a result of this. Next, she received inner cleansing as we washed off the negative emotions and unclean spirits, such as, shame, lust and perversion. I asked the Lord to delete all pornographic memories, from her conscious, subconscious and unconscious memory. As she came out of the spiritual cleansing pool, we asked Jesus if He would like to give her something in exchange. She saw Him giving her a robe of purity and righteousness. She commented how she felt cleansed, healed and set free from shame and defilement.

Sexual temptation is one of the battles of the mind to recognise and resist, and this involves having healthy boundaries and being accountable to others, hating the sin and pursuing an intimate relationship with Jesus.

END NOTES:

Some recommended reading;
a) Radmall, Bill: *Insight Into Addiction CWR (2009)*
b) Vallotton, Kris: *Purity: The New Moral Revolution (2008)*
c) Mulinde, John: *Set Apart For God: The call to a surrendered life (2005)*

13

Dealing With Fear & Control

Do not let your hearts be troubled. Trust in God; trust also in Me

John 14:1

Fear can affect us in different ways. Some may struggle with fear and anxiety more than others. Most fears are based on false beliefs and lies, and until we discern the truth behind every fear, the fear can keep us in bondage. Recognising fears and not partnering with them is a key to healing and freedom.

Usually, when we feel threatened, afraid or anxious, our body responds by producing adrenaline and other stress hormones. Adrenaline makes our heart beat faster to pump blood to our muscles to prepare us for a 'fight or flight' response. This is an appropriate response if we need to take action or avoid immediate harm or danger. However, many people have developed inappropriate anxieties and fears, based on traumas, false beliefs, insecurities and lies. Inappropriate fears and anxious responses can be triggered even when things appear to be safe.

Fear is seen to be strongly linked with control. When people feel they have lost control over something or someone, their response is one of anxiety or panic, until they regain control. This may be an appropriate or inappropriate response. For example, if a child is at sudden risk of being injured then the parent will take control to prevent the child being hurt or injured. Or if a person has looming exams and starts to get anxious, then they will take appropriate action (or control) by commencing their studies. However, when a person always has to be in control or is constantly anxious about things, then we are probably dealing with an ungodly stronghold. Let us take a look at the ungodly strongholds of fear and control.

Stronghold of Fear

Fear can be a natural, rational response to prevent something potentially harmful from happening. However, ongoing fears tend to become irrational and inappropriate, and are based on 'what ifs', 'lies' or 'false beliefs'.

Most of us fear something. There are those who accept fears as part of life and those who deny having any fears. However, fear is one of the enemy's weapons to keep us in bondage. This is because what we fear, we empower. Fear is Satan's very character and nature. Though fear is an emotion, it may also be a spirit. David said: *'I sought the Lord and He answered me; He **delivered** me from all **my fears**'* (Psalm 34:4). Paul said: *'God hasn't given us a **spirit of fear** but of power, love and a sound mind'* (2 Timothy 1:7). Here, Paul uses a different Greek word for fear[1] that is rarely used in the New Testament and means timidity, cowardice or backing off. In other words, Paul was saying *'God hadn't given you a spirit of cowardice or timidity, but of power…'*

Fear & Lies

Fears are actually based on lies. F.E.A.R is known as False Evidence Appearing Real. This is because it is based on a lie or false belief. Hence, we can ask God for the truth behind every fear, and replace the fear with His truth. His truth will set us free.

At one point in my life, unexpected things suddenly happened that made me feel not in control, and so I felt anxious about what my future held. When I asked the Lord what was behind my fear, I had a picture of an empty cloud. The fear appeared real like the outline of a cloud, but it was empty inside. Hence it was false evidence appearing real. The Lord revealed how He was in charge of my life and for me to simply put my trust in Him.

One of the reasons a fear may not leave with prayer is because we haven't told the *spirit* behind the fear to leave. Or it may be that we have renounced the spirit of fear, only to open ourselves to the same fear when faced with it again. This is probably because we haven't dealt with the *lie* attached to the fear.

Before I was about to serve in Africa, the enemy threw a massive fear my way and said, 'If you go, you will become infected with a virus and die!' Admittedly, the fear made me feel dreadful and not want to go, though I clearly knew this wasn't God's voice. I kept renouncing the fear but it kept coming back. I somehow couldn't shake it off. However, I finally overcame when I realized the fear was based on a lie. So I renounced the fear and put faith in God's truth spoken to my heart. God's truth was He would protect my life and even if I did contract some illness, He is the Lord who can heal me. I had to put my trust and faith in God to overcome this fear, which was based on a lie from the enemy. Once I held onto this truth and placed my faith in God, the fear went.

What we fear the most is probably our calling. It is interesting that the enemy made me fear contracting some deadly illness in Africa when God was calling me to serve Him there with the healing ministry.

The *Corona virus* outbreak in 2020 released a pandemic of fear through the news and social media. To overcome the fear we were to seek God's truth concerning the virus. Facts may change when they are based on man's opinion but His truth never changes. His truth quenches fear and puts things in the right perspective. Here are some examples of the things we may fear:

Fear of animals/insects
Fear of man/ commitment
Fear of isolation/ being alone/ poverty
Fear of rejection/not being wanted
Fear of the future/the unknown/ not being in control
Fear of flying/ heights/ closed or open spaces
Fear of letting go
Fear of failure/ disappointment
Fear of sickness/death/ hospitals

Fear of exposure/ shame/what others think or say about you
Fear of authorities
Fear of demons

Basically, we can fear anything, because fear is satan's weapon.

Roots to Fears
There can be different reasons why we may fear something and this depends on the roots to our fears. Firstly, fears may come from negative words or false beliefs that we have either read about or heard. These fears can come through books, adverts, papers, films, news, friends, family, or the social media. Secondly, fears may be rooted in negative experiences or traumas. Traumas and painful experiences involve negative thoughts and feelings and these generate fears. Thirdly, fears and anxieties may be passed down the bloodline. Since fear and anxiety can be passed to us from our parents and grandparents, we can receive a spirit of fear as early as the moment of conception.

For every fear, we can ask the Holy Spirit the reason or root behind the fear. Sometimes, we just have to exchange the false belief attached to the fear with His truth. However, in the case of a trauma or negative experience it will require inner healing from an encounter with Jesus. Once we renounce the fear and receive His healing, we can then exchange the lie behind the fear with His truth. His word is the truth that sets our hearts and minds free.

Ways to Overcome Fears

God has given us five weapons or tools to overcome fear. These are *love, faith, trust, peace,* and *truth*. These spiritual weapons are also the fruit of the Spirit.

Love Casts Out Fear
John the beloved, who was the disciple closest to Jesus, knew the Truth (John 14:6). He declared: *'There is no fear in love. But perfect love casts out fear'* (1 John 4:18). It is true that when we are filled with the love of God we have no fear. Many times, when I have been ministering to others, I have felt overwhelmed by His love to the extent it has quenched any fear of the demonic spirits manifesting. Satan operates from fear but God operates from love.

His Presence melts away all fear. Ungodly spirits shriek when they come into contact with anyone carrying God's love and Presence, because His love casts out all fear.

Faith & Trust Overcomes Fear
Fear tries to quench our spirit by attacking our faith. It aims to paralyse our emotions, hence the sayings, *'I froze with fear'* or *'I was scared stiff'*. Usually, what we fear the most is the very thing God is calling us to do. Hence, Satan tries to stop us obeying God's will with his arrows of fear. To obey God's calling requires stepping out in faith. Faith opposes fear! There is a saying: *'Fear knocked at the door but when faith opened the door, there was no-one there'*. Faith causes fear to flee. That is why it is like a shield, for it causes the arrows of fear to fall to the ground (Ephesians 6:16).

Many times we may not feel God's love when fear attacks our emotions but faith may be required instead. Jesus kept on telling His disciples: *'Do not fear! Have faith'*. When He calmed the storm, Jesus said to His disciples: *'Why are you so afraid? Do you still have no faith?'* (Mark 4:40). *'Do not worry about your life, what you will eat or drink…look at the birds of the air and how your heavenly Father feeds them…O you of little faith…But seek first His Kingdom and His righteousness and all these things will be given to you as well'* (Matthew 6:25-34).

During the time I served with Iris Global in a war-torn nation, I struggled to sleep when I heard noises in the night. The noises ranged from gunshots to beating of drums to abusive voices. One morning, as I was waking up in a sleepy, semi-conscious state, the Holy Spirit spoke clearly to my spirit. He said 'FAITH OVERCOMES FEAR'. I then realized in my spirit how fear is an emotion in our soul, but faith is a choice in our spirit. Our soul, which is part of our flesh, is to submit to our spirit. Faith doesn't rely on feelings but is a choice we make. The Holy Spirit went on to reveal the truth behind the fear of being attacked in the night. The truth was that God made the night for us to rest and let our mortal bodies sleep. It is His good will and intention for us to sleep, but the enemy tries to rob us of this truth with fears and lies that we are not safe and will be attacked. So I had to stop believing this lie and believe the truth that God was with me and would protect me in the night. I then prayed something like this before I went to sleep: *'Lord, keep every noise that is not of You from disturbing my sleep, but only if You want me to be woken up to pray, then wake me up'*. This worked and I slept with greater ease from then on, trusting my life in God's hands. He was faithful throughout my stay!

Faith can mean trusting in God. The more we grow closer to God, the more we put our trust in Him. Trust is about surrender. Hence, faith and trust are about surrendering our thoughts, feelings and will to God and not relying on our own understanding (Proverbs 3:5).

When we allow a spirit of fear to enter our hearts or minds, the enemy smells it and is attracted to it, because fear is like a bad odour. Demons are attracted to fear. Faith, on the other hand, is like a sweet fragrance which demons hate.

Peter walked on water as he stepped out in faith, because His eyes were focused on Jesus. When he took his eyes off Jesus and looked down at the raging waves, fear entered and he began to sink (Mathew 14:27-32). Fear comes when we take our eyes off Jesus. We overcome fear by turning our focus back to Him.

It takes faith to see what God is doing in the midst of a storm. It happened with Elisha when the king of Syria sent an army out to kill him. His servant was afraid of what he naturally saw, but Elisha told him not to fear, for those who were with them were more than those who were with the king's army. Elisha prayed that God would open his servant's eyes, and next he saw the hills full of horses and chariots of fire (2 Kings 6:15-17). We too can pray, *'Lord, open my eyes to see what You are doing in the Heavenly realms!'* As we start to see things through supernatural lenses and from God's perspective, it will release more faith. We should pray not from fear but rather from faith. If we look at things through our spiritual eyes and hearts focused on Jesus, we will overcome the fears the enemy tries to throw at us. Fear will tell us one thing but faith will say the opposite. Who are we choosing to believe and listen to?

Peace in Exchange for Fear
Natural peace is the absent of noise, whereas supernatural peace is the Presence of God. Peace is more than an inner state of being, for peace is a person. Jesus is the Prince of Peace. This is one of

His names along with Mighty God, Wonderful Counselor and Everlasting Father (Isaiah 9:6). Paul knew how the God of peace crushes Satan under our feet (Romans 16:20). This is because Christ reigns in the heavenly realms, above all rule, dominion, power and authority. As we rest in His Presence, He is with us. Therefore, when we rest in God's Presence with our eyes and hearts turned to Him, Satan is under our feet (Ephesians 1:20 + 2:6).

Jesus quenched His disciple's fear by saying: *'Peace be with you'* (John 20:19). Before He left His disciples He told them: *'Peace I leave with you; My peace I give you. Do not let your hearts be troubled and do not be afraid'* (John 14:27). God created us to live in peace, not fear. Usually when a spirit of fear leaves we receive God's peace. Worldly peace is the absence of noise or stress around us, but Godly peace is His Spirit resting in us.

'The Lord is near. **Do not be anxious about anything**, *but in everything by prayer and petition, with thanksgiving, present your requests to God.* **And the peace of God which transcends all understanding, will guard your hearts and minds** *in Christ'* (Philippians 4:4-7). We can choose whether to lean on Christ and give all our fears to Him, or allow anxious thoughts to infest our hearts and minds.

God is with us during our hardest moments in life. He will never leave us or desert us. He says: *'Fear not, for I have redeemed you; I have summoned you by name; you are Mine.* **When** *you pass through the waters, I will be with you; and* **when** *you pass through the rivers, they will not sweep over you.* **When** *you walk through the fire, you will not be burned; the flames will not set you ablaze. For I am the Lord your God, the Holy One of Israel, your Saviour'* (Isaiah 43:1-5). Do we believe this?

The moment I was asked to serve in a war-torn nation, I responded with fear. I was afraid of losing my life or being shot. When I asked the Lord if it was His will for me to serve Him in this nation, He instantly lifted the fear and gave me His peace. I knew He was saying yes, for His Presence was with me.

Psalm 23:4 says: *'Even though I walk through the valley of the shadow of death,* **I will fear no evil, for You are with me.** *Your rod and staff they comfort me'*. Even when facing death, or trials, or unknown situations, we have nothing to fear for God is with us.

Our faith and trust is to be totally in Him and not our situations or circumstances, or self. The safest place is in His Presence. If God is with us, then we do not need to be afraid.

Truth Quenches Lies and Fears
As already mentioned, fears are based on lies, so when dealing with fears we can ask God for His truth. God's truth is in His Living Word and Spirit. Jesus is the way, the truth and the life (John 14:6). Hence, we simply can ask Him for His truth. One of the best ways to do this is to write down our fears and negative thoughts. Then ask the Holy Spirit for His truth concerning each fear or negative thought. As we write down His truth, we can declare His truth over each fear and lie. His truth is like a sword that quenches every lie or fear from the enemy. From now on, we simply declare His truth instead of partnering with the lies.

God has given us the weapons of love, faith, trust, peace and truth to overcome every fear. All lies behind each fear can be replaced with the truth we hear from God. His word is truth. Once we renounce each fear, we can invite the Holy Spirit to fill us with His love and peace, as we choose to put our faith and trust in Him. Each time we declare His truth it quenches the spirit of fear. If the fear has been related to a traumatic experience, then we can invite Jesus into the memory to restore healing and freedom in our hearts.

Trauma & Fear
A spirit of fear usually enters a person during a traumatic event. Most of us have experienced some form of trauma. This may be trauma through a death, an accident, some form of abuse (verbal, physical or sexual) or some other event. For example, a person may fear dogs after having a dog bite, or fear driving after a car crash, or fear cancer after witnessing others die from cancer. The enemy tries to come at us with fear when we face a traumatic event, whether the trauma is in our own life or witnessed in the lives of others.

On one occasion, I was surprised when the Holy Spirit revealed I had a fear of death. On asking Him when this entered into my life, I had a picture of myself as a baby being delivered in my Mum's birth canal. It was dark and I got stuck, and couldn't get out. It was fairly traumatic. I then saw myself being pulled back into the light. On questioning my Mum, she said I did get stuck when she was trying to give birth and the doctor had to do an emergency caesarean section. So this fear of death came as a result of birth trauma. I repented and renounced the fear along with the spirit of trauma. Then I asked Jesus where He was during this moment, and I saw Him come into the situation and rescue me with His light. After seeing Him with me, I no longer had anything to fear. Fears can be exchanged with God's peace when we encounter Jesus in a trauma. The sense of fear can leave our memory as we see Him coming to our rescue, bringing His comfort, protection and peace.

It is important to realize there can be a spirit attached to the trauma. Just as there can be a spirit of fear, so there can be a *spirit of trauma*. Hence, we can address the spirit of trauma, as well as any other spirit that may have entered during a traumatic event. We can invite Jesus into the scene of the trauma, so we receive His healing and peace in exchange for the fear. When we are healed, we may still have the memory but no longer have the fear. In some traumas, where the memory may be quite graphic or the person is having flashbacks, then we can ask God to erase the memory of the scene, so the person may remember the event, but no longer remembers the graphic details.

We do not need to live with fears. We have a choice. As we recognize each fear we can ask Jesus to come into each situation and reveal His truth. The fear will go like a puff of wind when we receive His truth.

I met a lady who had a fear of hospitals. When her mum was admitted to the hospital, I offered to take her to see her mum, but she fearfully said she couldn't go. She didn't know why she had the fear. I prayed the Lord would deliver her from the fear. She had never stepped foot in a hospital. A day or so later, I heard she visited her mum. The Lord lifted her fear, and after her first visit she had no future problems with hospitals. Sometimes we have to face the fear head on to overcome it. Then we realise it wasn't such a giant after all, but rather a mouse we can tread on (Psalm 91:13). Inappropriate fear blows things well out of proportion to the truth, since it is *false evidence appearing real.*

Ignore the Demons

Many people may fear demons, especially if they manifest at night. Some may have rebuked the spirits or prayed in tongues, and still nothing happened. Smith Wigglesworth gave a testimony of a memorable experience. One night he encountered a red demon at the foot of his bed and it tried to frighten him. In response he said something like, *'Oh it's only you'* and turned over in his bed. He ignored the demon and fell back to sleep. The demon never appeared again.

Demons carry fear and try to imprison us with their fear. We empower demons when we respond to their fear. That means we have accepted what they carry, that is, the spirit of fear. However, if we ignore their fear, then we render them powerless and in effect they are made redundant. Sometimes, the right thing may be to ignore demons when they try to attack us, so we do not receive or empower their fear.

Fear of Being Attacked by Man

One day, I came under a fear of being attacked, when a lecturer planted the thought that there was a high chance of being attacked in Africa because I was a single woman. Because I believed this lie, it meant I gave the enemy legal access or an open door in my heart to inflict this fear.

Years later, the Lord highlighted this fear, and so I repented of this fear and renounced the spirit behind it. Then I asked Jesus to come and reveal His truth. He gave me this picture. I saw myself dressed as a bride with a sword in my hand and army boots on my feet. Next, I saw the enemy in the form of a violent-looking, bald headed man with chains and tattoos over his body, trying to come and physically attack me. Then, I raised my sword in the Name of Jesus, and the enemy suddenly stopped and could move no further. Jesus said He has given us power and authority to overcome *all power* of the enemy. We have nothing to fear. Behind the fear was the lie that as a woman I was vulnerable to the power of men. The disciples told Jesus that even the demons submit to them in His Name. He replied: *'I have given you authority to trample on snakes and scorpions and to* **overcome all the power of the enemy; nothing will harm you'** (Luke 10:19).

Evil people carry evil spirits. Though we may not have the physical power to stop such evil, we do have the power of the Holy Spirit. Demonic spirits have to submit to the Spirit of God in us. I held onto the truth that He who is in us is greater than him in the world (1 John 4:4).

Stronghold of Control

There may be situations in everyday life when we are to take control to prevent unwanted circumstances arising. However, appropriate control is different from a spirit that *always wants to* or *needs to* be in control. Control becomes a stronghold when it is regularly used for means to gain power. Those who have a *spirit of control* struggle when they are not in control. The spirit of control *always* wants to be in charge, whether to control others or things, so that everything is done *their way*. Some may use verbal, physical or demonic power as means to gain control. Others may take control in a subtle, non-threatening but more manipulative manner. Likewise, people may become victims to the control of others. People may be controlled and intimidated by their bosses, leaders, friends or spouses.

Wanting to always be in control or use power-control, will restrict and quench the move of the Holy Spirit. When a person feels in control over their environment or others, it gives them a sense of power. However, the more we do things in our own strength and power, the less we depend on God's Spirit and power. Jesus did everything in the power of the Spirit for He said: *'The Son can do nothing by Himself; He can do only what He sees His Father doing,'* (John 5:19). God will empower those who seek His will and choose to depend on His Spirit.

Our thoughts behind the need or want to be in control are usually based on a lie, since they are linked to fear. We may think, *'Unless I do it, it won't happen. No-one else can do it to my standard, so I have to do it'*. Or, *'I need to tell them my opinion so they do what I think is best'*. The truth is, sometimes we simply have to let go or let others do things their way. The Lord wants us to give the control reins in our heart over to Him, and let Him be in charge. This means putting our trust in Him as we choose to depend more on Him.

Control is not to be confused with *'self-control'* which is a fruit of the Spirit. This is when we take control over our 'self'. This means control of our actions, tongue and emotions, by restraining ourselves from doing things we may regret. We are to have self-control over our own body, soul and spirit but this is quite different from wanting to take control over others.

Control & False Responsibility

Sometimes, there may be a spirit of false responsibility linked with control. This is when we may feel responsible for a person or group (or something), and the need to be in control. Instead, we should be open to what the Holy Spirit is saying in our lives. The truth may be we are not the one to take responsibility in this given situation and instead let someone else take responsibility.

While I was leading a medical team on the mission field, I felt responsible for the actions the team took concerning the treatment of patients. So I would check up on them to see if they were making the right diagnosis and decisions. At the conscious level, this seemed the right thing to be doing. However, there was an underlying fear that if they made a mistake, I would be to blame, so I felt responsible for the decisions they made. It was then brought to my attention through a fellow colleague that I was operating under a spirit of fear and control, along with a spirit of false responsibility. This was a huge lesson for me. The truth was my colleagues were not my responsibility. I had to let them make mistakes so they could learn from them, and I had to learn to not fear the consequences. I had to let go of the reins of control and hand them to the team so they had more freedom to operate. This seemed scary at first but was ultimately freeing for myself, as well as the team. Instead of carrying the weight of false responsibility, I had to make myself hold back and be available for the team to approach me if they had questions or needed help. In all this, I learnt that a good leader is one who can facilitate a team, instead of one who tries to control from the top.

Control & Fear

As already mentioned, control is linked to fear. We start to fear when we no longer feel in control. The fear makes us try and get control again over our situation and becomes a vicious circle of fear-control-fear-control. To get control we may shout or express anger through *power-control*. Others start to *panic* when they feel out of control. It's important to recognise the change of tone in voice when power-control manifests through anger or rage. The person can ask Jesus why they reacted like this, and what is the root to the fruit of their anger? Likewise, instead of reacting to a situation with panic or fear, we can choose to put our trust in God and give Him the reins of control. Holding onto control will cause bondage, but releasing control can bring freedom.

God doesn't control us, but He has given us the free will to choose. He will tell us what is right and wrong, but gives us the free will to make decisions. There are consequences when we choose to disobey and rewards when we choose to obey. This is a Kingdom principle. Likewise, we are to offer choices to others instead of trying to get them to do what we want. A good leader or parent is someone who leads, not by a spirit of rulership or control, but a willingness to let others make decisions through offering choices. This may mean releasing responsibility to others and allowing them to make mistakes. It is not about proving ourselves to be better than others. Instead, we are to encourage, disciple and empower others.

Control & Manipulation

Control may partner with the spirit of manipulation. Manipulation is when we try to get people to do what we want them to do. Control used with manipulation is a form of witchcraft and comes with a degree of deception. Either the person operating behind the manipulation is unaware they are doing this, or they are aware but do things in such a way that others are unaware they are being manipulated.

Manipulation is when someone says or does something that appears to be in the other person's interest but is actually in their own interest all along. Their motive is hidden and self-promoting. Manipulation is cunning and devious. It tries to get a person to do what it wants them to in such a way that it looks like it is doing it for the other person's interest. In essence, it is also a form of dishonesty for it does not want to admit the real reason or motive behind the gesture given.

People may try and make it look like they have your best interests at heart when really they only have their own. We see this between King Darius and his administrators. When Darius became pleased with Daniel and wanted him to rule over the whole kingdom, the other administrators became jealous for they wanted to rule themselves. So they suggested to the king to enforce a decree where the people were to worship him and no other god for a period of thirty days. If anyone was caught praying to another god, he was to be thrown into the lions' den. This seemed to be in the king's interest, yet all along it was a set-up to put Daniel in the lions' den (Daniel 6:3-9). A spirit of discernment is required to be able to recognise hidden motives so we do not succumb to the enemy's plan. We are not to judge by what we see or hear, but discern in our spirit what is the truth behind each given situation (Isaiah 11:3).

When manipulation plays on the emotions, it is known as *emotional manipulation*. People may get others to do what they want through playing on their emotions, such as crying, or the self-pity 'woe is me' talk, or a victim mindset. Or there may be *sensual manipulation,* as was the case with Delilah when she used sexual temptations to get what she wanted from Samson (Judges 16). Others may use threatening speech or intimidate people as a means to get people to do what they want. Manipulation is also seen through bribes, where people give or promise something only if others will do something in return. We are to avoid every kind of manipulation, and rebuke the spirit behind it.

Shame, Fear & Control
Shame is a feeling of humiliation and loss of dignity. People may feel shame when they struggle to forgive themselves for something they have done or not done. Or a sense of shame may be *perceived* because of what others say about us. For example, some may feel ashamed about their physical looks, disabilities, or where they live, because of the humiliating and intimidating words spoken by others. People who have been abused will often carry shame because they falsely believe it was their fault or they were to blame.

The good news is there is no shame in the Kingdom. It is not in God's dictionary because it is Satan's language. One day while I was worshipping, I heard the words, 'There is no shame in the Kingdom'. I realised in my spirit that shame is from the enemy, for he is out to accuse, humiliate and intimidate everyone. Shame puts us in bondage. Hence, as we receive God's healing and forgiveness, we can be freed from shame. The Lord wants us to be free from all shame along with any guilt that goes with it. Guilt and shame can be like dirty marks on our clothes. When a child comes to their parent with dirty clothes, and then apologizes or explains what happened, the parent will lovingly remove their clothes and give them new or clean clothes to wear. How much more will our Heavenly Father forgive our sins and cleanse us, when we come to Him with sorrowful hearts. His love never changes.

When God forgives, He remembers our sins no more (Jeremiah 31:34). Shame is built on negative thoughts and lies from the enemy. Once we are forgiven or have forgiven ourselves, then we can receive His words of truth that release freedom. All that matters is what God says about us and how He sees us. This truth is what we hold onto and not what others may think or say. *'No-one whose hope is in God will ever be put to shame'* (Psalm 25:2). This is what God says: *'Instead of their shame My people will receive a double portion, and instead of their disgrace they will rejoice in their inheritance'* (Isaiah 61:7).

Shame can be linked to fear and control. When we have done something that makes us feel ashamed, we may fear what others will think if they find out. This makes us feel the need to act and take control by doing something to stop this happening. When we are ashamed of our actions or response, then this requires repentance as we come before God. Once we address the shame we become free from the fear and control. God wants to set us free from any shame linked to fear and control.

The best example of shame being linked to fear and control is when David committed adultery with Bathsheba. When she became pregnant, David tried to cover up the evidence for fear her husband would find out, so he took control by ordering her husband to return home and enjoy time with his wife. When her husband refused to leave his fellow men, David arranged for him to be put on the front line in battle. Since he feared this happening, he took control by ordering Bathsheba's husband to be put on the front line with the chance of being killed in battle. A prophet convicted David of what he had done. After he wholeheartedly repented, God forgave his sin and removed his shame (2 Samuel 11+12).

There was a case where a mother felt ashamed when she heard that her daughter had become pregnant. Since her daughter was not married, she feared what others would think or say, about her and also her daughter. She felt she had failed as a mother, and as a result tried to take control over the situation. However, during a time of ministry, she chose to give her feelings of shame, fear and control, to Jesus. In exchange, the Lord revealed she had a loving mother's heart, and removed her guilt and shame. She no longer feared what others thought. All that mattered was what the Lord thought and had revealed to her heart.

Jesus Sets an Example

Jesus never took control over his disciples. Instead, He gave them free will to follow Him. Many chose to leave Him after He said they were to eat His flesh and drink His blood. He asked His twelve if they were going to leave Him too (John 6:60-70). He never bribed them, but spoke of the riches and rewards for those who did His Father's will.

He let them loose to experiment on healing as He entrusted them with His authority and power. God knows our strengths and weaknesses. He allows us to make mistakes in order to learn from them. He sees our mistakes before we do, yet He still loves us.

Jesus saw Peter's potential, yet rebuked the spirit of control that was displayed when Peter feared Jesus' death. Peter said: *'Never Lord! This shall never happen to You!'* Then Jesus replied: *'Get thee behind Me, Satan! You are a stumbling block to Me; you do not have in mind the things of God but the things of men'* (Mathew 16:21-23). Peter displayed a spirit of control linked to his fear. Hence, Jesus rebuked the spirit in Peter for it was trying to prevent Him doing God's will. Control actually hinders spiritual growth and limits the work of the Spirit. Whereas free will allows us to make mistakes and gives greater room for growth.

Ways to Overcome Control

Here are some ways to help us overcome the spirit of control.

Surrender the Control Reins to God
The hardest thing for a controlling person to do is to give the control reins to God. This is because we struggle to put our trust in God, or think we can do a better job without the need of others or God. However, we are to trust in the Lord with *all* our heart and not lean on our own understanding. In *everything* we are to acknowledge Him, and He will make our paths straight (Proverbs 3:3-6). Each time we surrender the reins of control, we are choosing to depend on Him. The Lord doesn't demand this from us, but lovingly and graciously asks us to let go, so we may learn to co-labour with Him as we yield to the move of His Spirit.

Seek His Ways & Truth
Instead of believing the fears attached to the spirit of control, we can choose to seek His ways and thoughts for each given situation. Whereas fears and lies keep us in bondage, His truth releases freedom. '*"For My thoughts are not your thoughts, neither are your ways My ways," declares the Lord'* (Isaiah 55:8). Hence, we can ask for His Spirit of truth to guide us in His ways concerning each area of responsibility (John 14:17+ 26).

Submission to Leadership
One of the ways to overcome the spirit of control is the willingness to submit to others, especially those in leadership. (I am referring to healthy leadership and not unhealthy leadership where the leader is controlling or manipulative to others). This mustn't be a false submission that is seeking power, but a true unconditional yielding, being willing to serve. True submission is when we are willing to do things we don't really want to do. Likewise, submission to God's will means being willing to let go of our will and give the control reins to God. This is not walking away from responsibility, but trusting in His will and guidance concerning everything. This can play an important part in our spiritual growth.

HEALING TOOLS

Dealing with Familial Spirits

As already mentioned, the controlling spirit may be passed down the bloodline through our parents and grandparents. During a season of timeout, there were moments when I would feel frustrated, not understanding why God was holding me back when it seemed obvious that I should be using my gifts on the mission field. I couldn't understand, until someone pointed out, that my frustration was due to not feeling in control. There was a fear that I was not doing what I should be doing and the lie that I was wasting my time doing nothing. Whenever my friends prayed and gave me words of encouragement, the peace of God would return and the frustration would lift. However, the peace only lasted a week or so, until the frustration would return again. I somehow didn't seem to be free from it. When I asked for prayer, it was interesting what transpired. The reason the frustration kept returning was because it was a familial spirit of control which I hadn't yet broken. When the Holy Spirit gave further revelation on the matter, I was able to forgive my parents, repent of the sin and break myself free from it once and for all. An amazing peace came upon me, as well as a revelation of the truth that my timeout was a significant season in my journey with God that would map my future. It was important I came to know His ways and this included being able to tabernacle His Presence. Since then, I have come to a deeper awareness of His Presence, having realized He was preparing me for something new in His Kingdom.

There are different branches or manifestations that come from the stronghold of control and these can present in various ways. It is a process to overcome the spirit of control as the Holy Spirit exposes the various ways it may manifest in our daily life. The key is to ask Jesus how He would respond in each given situation, and then rewire our minds with His ways of thinking, as we respond not by might but by His Spirit (Zechariah 4:6).

Sicknesses Linked to Control

Some illnesses or symptoms may be rooted to a spirit of control, especially if there is any witchcraft involved. I have seen many people become sick or develop symptoms as a result of witchcraft.

Once the power of witchcraft is broken in Jesus' name, the symptoms go.

A missionary colleague was regularly becoming ill with one symptom after another. She would be healed of something, only to fall sick with something else. In the majority of cases, I believed it was due to the effects of witchcraft. Each time I prayed for her and broke the power of witchcraft, her symptoms would instantly go.

I met a woman who had struggled with the eating disorder known as anorexia nervosa. Her aversion to food was based on a spirit of self-hate and the need to take control over what she ate. She had no control over her life for her parents did everything and were quite controlling in different ways. The only part where she felt in control was with what she ate. However, this wasn't a healthy 'self-control,' but rather an obsessive control that caused her body to suffer. Once she received healing in these areas, her eating returned to normal and she was able to regain weight.

The spirit of control, like any other ungodly spirit, can affect the spirit, soul and body. Some may suffer with physical and spiritual bondage as a result of coming under a controlling spirit.

Stress Related Illnesses (based on fear-control)
Many illnesses are stress based due to an underlying anxiety or fear. Stress is a symptom not a diagnosis. It is well known that stress and anxiety cause negative effects on our body. Stress may precipitate stomach ulcers from increased acid production, asthmatic problems from constriction of the airways, headaches or angina from hypertension, irritable or inflammatory bowel symptoms, muscle aches and body fatigue (chronic myalgia or fatigue syndrome) skin problems (like eczema), allergies and mental health issues. Basically, stress can affect or attack any part of our body. Hence we need to recognize this so we don't dampen down the symptoms with suppressive medication, but rather minimize it by changing our mindset or lifestyle so we are no longer letting our bodies suffer from the physical, mental or emotional effects of stress or anxiety.

Stress related symptoms are like a wake-up call. We are to deal with what's causing the stress instead of trying to treat the symptoms. Hence, medication for asthma, eczema, headaches, high blood pressure, acid-reflux, exhaustion, mental health issues and so on, do not cure but rather suppress the symptoms by dampening them down.

Anxiety and stress may be due to fears, negative thoughts, not feeling in control or too many burdens. We may be struggling to lean on God and give Him our burdens. Only when we learn to lean on Him, our burdens become lighter as we give the control reins to Him. The more we surrender to Him, the more we will be able to walk in His grace to help us through whatever we are facing.

The world teaches us to do things our own way, to strive to be the best and use our own strength and abilities. Yet Jesus taught something different. He said we are to lean on Him and not our own understanding, and commit all our plans or ideas to Him, just as He did with the Father (Proverbs 3:5, Proverbs 16:3, John 5:19). He said we are to do things not by might or by strength but by His Spirit (Zechariah 4:6). This becomes more natural as we spend time with Him and get to know Him deeper in our hearts. Instead of living with the fears and lies from the enemy, we can live with His peace and truth.

God gives us His peace and grace when we are in His will, even if we happen to be facing the valley of the shadow of death, or the storms in life. We were not created to walk it alone but with Him. We can choose to do things our way or seek God's help and do it His way. His way is always the best.

END-NOTES

[1] Deilia (Greek 1167): *Strong's Expansive Exhaustive Concordance, Red Letter Edition*

14

Unbelief & False Beliefs

If I am telling the truth, why don't you believe Me?
He who belongs to God hears what God says

John 8: 45-47

Most Christians, knowingly or unknowingly, struggle with unbelief and false beliefs. Unbelief is different to false belief. Unbelief is based on having no belief or a lack of faith in God's power and authority. False belief is based on having some belief, but not necessarily the right belief. Many of us have false beliefs simply because we lack God's truth on an issue or when we fail to see things from God's perspective. False beliefs, either about ourselves, God or others, may keep us in bondage until we seek the truth concerning these beliefs. God's truth is a spiritual weapon (Ephesians 6:14). It is a sword because as we declare His word of truth, it breaks us free from bondage (John 17:17). It is His Spirit of truth that sets us free (John 8:32).

Unbelief

Jesus was unable to heal many in His hometown because of their lack of faith or unbelief (Mathew 13:58, Mark 6:5-6). When Jesus was asked to heal the fitting boy, the boy's father said: *'If you can do anything, take pity on us and help us,'* to which Jesus replied: *'"If you can", everything is possible to him who believes.'* And the man replied; *'I do believe; help me overcome my unbelief!'* (Mark 9:22-24).

The Greek word for unbelief is *Apistia* [1] and means faithlessness. James says the prayer offered in faith will make the sick person well (James 5:15). However, we must be careful not to accuse or judge a person who is not healed by saying it was *their* lack of faith. The truth is the faith of the person praying for the sick can release healing as we see throughout scriptures. Likewise, I have seen people healed when I have lacked faith, or not healed when I have had faith.

Healing is an act of God's grace, so let's be careful not to condemn people by saying it's their lack of faith or unresolved sin. God can still heal those who have no faith or who live in sin. However, healing is witnessed more where there is repentance of sin and a release of faith. People can have faith and not get healed, or have no faith and get healed. At times, God's healing is not as straightforward as we would like to think it is.

One way to release faith is to ask the person if they believe in God, and if so, do they believe He can heal them. If they say yes, then we can pray through the eyes of faith (or with a sanctified imagination) that the person with the sick part of their body is healed. This was my approach when ministering to people of other faiths on the islands of Mozambique and it seemed to work in most cases.

When we pray by faith, we can thank God for healing someone and then let the person test out the affected part of their body. Faith put in action releases healing. I noticed that those who tested their bodies to see if they were healed were more likely to see healing compared to those who didn't. If the person has improved, even just a little, I would pray again thanking God for the healing. Each time I prayed and asked God to complete what He had started, more healing would be witnessed by the person.

God of the Impossible
Many of us do not believe that God is the God of the impossible. If we did, then we would laugh at the impossible, knowing all things are possible with God. However, we tend to accept the doctor's diagnosis or remarks, instead of turning to God to ask Him what He thinks. Or some may *try* prayer but if it doesn't seem to work, they quickly give up and try something else. God

can heal anything for He is the God of miracles. Nothing is too difficult for Him. Jesus kept saying: *'Have faith! Believe! Do not doubt! Do not fear!'* Everything God created, including you and me, is a miracle. Nature is a miracle. Natural healing is a miracle. How can a tree grow from a seed? How can a human grow from a sperm and ova? Medicine *assists* the process of natural healing. Jesus said we start with faith like the size of a mustard seed. The more we step out, our faith will begin to grow. God responds to those who live by faith. God created us to live naturally supernatural lives, just like Jesus did. Our faith isn't to be in man or ourselves but in Him, because He is the One who heals and sets us free.

When the disciples asked Jesus why they couldn't heal the fitting boy, He replied: *'It was because of your lack of faith. I promise you, if you have faith inside of you no bigger than the size of a small mustard seed, you can say to this mountain, 'Move away from here and go over there' and you will see it move! There is nothing you couldn't do!'* (TPT Matthew 17:20). Other translations read: *'Nothing is impossible for you!'* Jesus is emphasizing the power of us having faith in God, because with faith, nothing is impossible.

Faith but still no Healing

There will be some thinking, *'Yes but what about those who have faith and keep on praying but still see no results?'* I have tried to explain some possible reasons why people may not be healed in the chapter *'Blockages to Healing'* in Volume One. However, there will always be cases where no matter what we do or who we go to for ministry, a person remains unhealed or even dies. Quite often there are things we can't see that only God sees. Sometimes, we just aren't ready for the revelation. Jesus had much more He wanted to teach and reveal to His disciples, but they weren't ready for it. *'I have much more to say to you, more than you can bear,'* (John 16:12).

Sometimes, it may be we have to contend for a spiritual breakthrough before seeing healing. However, we must never give up, even if a person dies. Many have received an anointing to heal in a specific area of ministry, but this has come through persistent prayer and after contending for breakthrough.

False Beliefs

We all have false beliefs where we believe things to be true when they are actually false. This is when we fail to see things from God's perspective or don't seek His truth on an issue. False beliefs can be about anything. The greatest example is seen in government, where one Member of Parliament strongly believes one thing and another Member of Parliament disagrees and believes the opposite is true. Someone is wrong and someone is right, yet everyone believes they are right. We can have false beliefs concerning ourselves, God or others. False beliefs come from negative experiences, listening to man's opinion, and following the wisdom of this world.

A false belief is based on man's opinion or a false interpretation of things, instead of the truth from the Spirit. False beliefs can affect our health and relationships. We all have some skewed views about God because of our upbringing and 'inherited beliefs'. Sometimes, the Holy Spirit may bring to mind a memory in childhood that created a false belief. For example, you may believe you can't trust anyone because of an experience you had when young. Or you may believe that you can't swim in the sea because you were told you will be eaten by a shark. Or you may believe no-one would like you if they knew the real you. These are just a few examples of how our experiences or worldly beliefs create false beliefs, until we hear God's truth for each case.

There are many things we have believed about ourselves that are simply not true, for they are not from God. If we are not careful, the false beliefs or negative words we speak over ourselves may become self-fulfilling prophecies. The source of false beliefs and lies is Satan, the father of lies (John 8:44). Satan delights in telling us we are no good, not wanted, will never make it, must strive for success, God isn't bothered about us, God can't see what we're doing, God doesn't heal, God is angry with us, God will leave us, and so on. He doesn't want us to know the truth, because the truth sets us free (John 8:32). Lies and false beliefs defile our hearts and minds. Jesus prayed that we would be *sanctified* by the truth, because His Word is truth (John 17:17). Jesus sent us His Spirit of Truth to guide us in all things (John

14:17). This emphasizes the importance of seeking His truth in daily things, so that we may stay on His path of Life. And Jesus is the Way, the Truth and the Life (John 14: 6).

God believes in us, even if no one else does. God has amazing plans and destinies for us. We simply are to ask the Holy Spirit to reveal the lies we have believed about ourselves or God or others. One way to do this is to ask the Holy Spirit to highlight the false beliefs and write each false belief down. Next, ask the Holy Spirit, 'What is the truth? How does God really see me? What does God say about this?' Then write down each truth as the words come to mind. The Lord may speak through His written word in the scriptures, or reveal His truth through His Spirit. We now have a choice- to either believe the lie/false belief or accept God's truth. What or who are we choosing to believe? God usually speaks His truth though His Word. This may be the written word or a *rhema* word breathed by His Spirit.

Studies have apparently shown that it takes about four weeks for a negative thought or false belief to be unwired from the brain and to rewire the brain with a positive thought or true belief. As we declare each truth for a period of four weeks or more, it then becomes wired or ingrained in our thought pattern. And this helps us to live life more abundantly when we believe in His truth.

Some believe Jesus doesn't want to heal them and they are to live with their sickness or problem. This simply isn't true. When we open our lives to sin, we are also opening ourselves up to sickness and disease that can come through sin (Exodus 15:26, Luke 13:16, Acts 10:38). It is also true that not all sickness and disease are due to sin. Jesus taught this to His disciples when He was questioned about the man born blind. He said the man was born blind not through any sin, but so the works of God could be displayed (John 9:1-3).

We have a choice. We can choose to live in the truth of how God sees us or choose to accept the lies based on how Satan sees us. One leads to freedom and the other to bondage. Since Jesus is the Truth, we can always come to Him when seeking His truth. When we ask by faith, He will always respond with His truth.

HEALING TOOLS

Many current 'beliefs' are the result of lies attached to negative experiences during childhood or from the words spoken by others. There can be fears attached to the lies. The Lord may bring back a memory of a painful event, so He can bring healing to the person and reveal the truth behind the painful memory. He reveals His truth to replace the lies, and this releases healing and freedom to the body, soul and spirit.

Many may suffer with unnecessary depression or oppression. This is like a dark cloud hovering over someone and following them where they go. It is usually based on false beliefs and lies that a person may have accumulated or inherited. If you listen to a depressed person, everything sounds negative because they see things through negative lenses. However, if the person writes down their negative beliefs and then asks the Holy Spirit for the truth, things start to shift. The brain is to be rewired with the truth about God and themselves, as they start to see things from God's perspective. The dark cloud starts to disperse as the truths are revealed and the way of thinking changes. Inner healing may be required if there has been rejection, broken relationships, grief or trauma, where the negative beliefs have become attached to wounded emotions.

There was a woman who was feeling down and oppressed after her daughter died of a chronic illness. She described feeling a sense of heaviness, like a dark cloud looming over her. So we prayed and asked the Holy Spirit to shine His light on any false beliefs and lies linked to her symptoms of grief. She wrote down a list of negative thoughts, such as, 'I could have done something to prevent her dying', 'It's my fault she was born with the illness,' and so on. Then we asked the Holy Spirit to reveal His truth concerning each negative belief. The response was amazing. When she read out the truths, she instantly saw the lies she had come under, and chose to reject the lies and hold on to God's truths concerning the death of her daughter. The dark cloud dispersed and was no longer over her.

In another situation, there was a young woman who was about to get married when her husband-to-be decided not to turn up on their wedding day. She was devastated to say the least, since he gave no warning and she never heard from him again.

From this she developed false beliefs and lies about herself and God. She thought there must be something wrong with her, and how could God have allowed this to happen? There were many negative thoughts that polluted her heart and mind. During a time of prayer, as she wrote down her negative thoughts and hurt emotions, the Lord lovingly revealed the truth concerning what had happened. For the first time, she saw it all from God's perspective and realized she wasn't to blame, and God had someone better for her. This was the beginning of her healing process as she started to see things from God's perspective.

One of the keys to overcoming false beliefs and man's opinion is to seek God's perspective on things. All we have to do is to simply ask God what He thinks and believes. Remember, His ways are not our ways, and His thoughts are not our thoughts (Isaiah 55:8).

True and False Guilt

Many people struggle to be set free where there's guilt involved. Guilt may be true or false and is usually linked to a feeling of responsibility. Guilt can imprison, hence God wants us to be set free from the bondage of guilt. When God forgives, He has forgiven indeed and remembers our sin or guilt no more (Jeremiah 31:34). The enemy is the one who keeps accusing us night and day, saying we haven't been forgiven and should feel guilty. Once we have been forgiven (or have forgiven ourselves), the enemy has no legal foothold to accuse us. We simply ignore these thoughts, knowing he is out to kill, steal and destroy, for he is the accuser of the brethren (Revelation 12:10). All we are to know is God's truth and what He says. His truth not only heals, but it sets us free.

True guilt is when someone is guilty for something. I may be guilty if I've stolen money or said I would do something and then didn't. On the other hand, false guilt is when a person is made to feel guilty for something when they are not at fault. For example, a person may be expected to do something for someone, when they didn't actually agree to do it. False guilt can be linked to false responsibility. A relative or friend may expect me to do something for them which I hadn't agreed to and hence make me feel guilty for not doing it. So I may feel pressured to do something that wasn't my responsibility in the first place.

True guilt requires repentance and receiving forgiveness from God. Sometimes we may need to forgive ourselves for what we did. Where there is true repentance from the heart, the Lord will instantly remove any guilt. In the case of false guilt, we also need to repent for coming under a *spirit of false guilt* and *false responsibility*. This may be the result of unhealthy soul-ties that probably need to be broken. Instead, we can develop healthy boundaries in our relationships, where it becomes normal to say 'no' or 'I'm sorry I can't...'

A woman I met believed many lies about herself and God as a result of the words spoken to her as a child. She was made to feel guilty for things that were not her fault. It sounded very much like Cinderella and her wicked step-mother. Instead of receiving love and encouragement, she was brought up receiving words of intimidation, blame and fear. She could never please her mother or do anything right no matter how hard she tried. One by one, she dealt with her childhood memories, as each lie and false guilt was exchanged for the Father's words of Truth and how He saw her. She chose to no longer partner with her negative thoughts based on fears and false guilt. Instead of being a Cinderella, she has become a warrior princess as she has discovered her true identity as a daughter of the King.

The closer we walk with God, the more we will come to understand His ways and thoughts. We can always look to Jesus for the truth, because He will always reveal it to us. He is the Truth and His truth sets us free (John 14:6).

END-NOTES

[1] Apostia (Greek 570); *Strong's Expanded Exhaustive Concordance, RedLetterEdition(2001).*

15

The Occult & Freemasonry

A number who had practiced sorcery brought their scrolls together and burned them publicly

Acts 19:19

The effects of witchcraft, freemasonry or involvement with the occult, may cause physical and mental illness, or even premature death. Many people go to 'faith healers', 'traditional healers', 'alternative therapists' or 'spirit masters' to seek healing, and believe the source of power must be good if they get better. However, people who call themselves faith healers, alternative therapists, spirit masters or traditional healers, may be using a source of 'healing power' that is not from God. By coming under this power, we are opening ourselves up to the demonic realm and are now at risk of accidents, ill health, mental issues or even premature deaths. Scripture warns us about false healers and false prophets who perform miracles: '*Then I saw* **another beast** *coming out of the earth. He* **performed great and miraculous signs**, *even causing fire to come down from heaven. Because of the signs...***he deceived the inhabitants of the earth***' (Revelation 13:11-14).

Satan's mission is to deceive us. We may open ourselves to the demonic realm through connecting to a source that looks good or a friend says is good, but isn't from God. And when we do this, then consequences may follow. Saul consulted a 'medium' to enquire about the battle with the Philistine Army. Shortly after this, he was killed in battle because he had opened a door to the enemy, and the spirit of death followed him (1 Samuel 28:1-24).

The Occult

The word 'occult' actually means 'hidden evil'. This includes 'secret societies' (such as freemasonry, buffaloes, orange lodge, mormonism, eastern religions, and so on) whose evil powers are hidden from the general public. Many have got involved with the occult without realizing this. The occult is a subtle way to open ourselves up to the demonic realm. It is hidden or undercover, for it comes in a deceptive manner. What appears to be a game or a bit of fun is really a gateway or access for demons to enter someone's life. Examples of this include taking part in things such as, palm reading, tarot cards, ouiji board, tea-leaf reading, séances, story books on witchcraft, dungeons and dragons, divining rods, psychic healing, mediums, crystal balls, clairvoyance and the list goes on.

If we have opened ourselves up to the demonic realm through any occult activity or form of witchcraft, then it's wise to close these doors to prevent any demonic activity further influencing our lives. *'Let no-one be found among you who sacrifices his son or daughter in the fire, who practices divination or sorcery, interprets omens, engages in witchcraft, or casts spells, or who is a medium or spiritist or who consults the dead. Anyone who does these things is detestable to the Lord'* (Deuteronomy 18:10-12).

Jesus forewarned His disciples there would be many coming claiming to be the Christ, and there would be anti-Christs and false prophets who would perform great signs and miracles to deceive God's people (Matthew 24:24). Just because someone is healed or a miracle happens doesn't mean it was from God. Jesus said: *'Not everyone who says to Me, "Lord, Lord" will enter the Kingdom of Heaven but only he who does the will of My Father who is in Heaven. Many will say to Me on that day, "Lord, Lord, did we not prophesy in Your Name and in Your Name drive out demons and perform many miracles?" Then I will tell them plainly, "I never knew you. Away from Me you evil doers!"'* (Matthew 7:21-23).

'Rebellion is like the sin of divination' (1 Samuel 15:23). When we rebel against God we are at risk of opening ourselves up to the sin of divination or witchcraft. Jesus told the crippled man to stop sinning if he wanted to stay healed because disobedience may lead to sickness and disease.

Sickness may be the result of past (including generational sins) or present involvement with the occult, or other sources of witchcraft including freemasonry. When medical tests have come back normal or appear to not show anything, I have questioned if there was possibly a spiritual or emotional root to the problem. If it seems to be appropriate, then I may ask if there was any involvement with witchcraft, freemasonry or dabbling in the occult. Even if a person hasn't directly been involved in the occult, they may be affected through the sins of their forefathers, or they may be under a curse inflicted by another person who dabbles in the occult.

Satan counterfeits all sicknesses. That is, for every real sickness and disease there can be counterfeit symptoms too. This is when things appear to be real but are actually counterfeit, hence medical tests come back normal. It's not that the person is faking it but rather their symptoms are of a spiritual origin. We have the authority in Christ to break all power and effects of witchcraft on human life.

Those who practice divination gain their knowledge from the demonic realm, and this includes psychic prediction or ESP (Extra Sensory Perception). The slave girl in Acts 16:16-22 is a good example of someone who was possessed with a spirit of divination. Psychic people or fortune tellers may carry a python spirit or other ungodly spirits that enable them to see into the past and future, but only from the demonic realm and not from God's heavenly realm. People may use the spirit of divination as a means to find where sickness is in bodies. This is seen with reflexology, iridology and other alternative medicines.

Sorcery is the demonstration of magical or demonic powers through incantations, blood sacrifices, charms and potions. It accesses power to bring people under the control of witchcraft, as well as invoking sickness, curses and death.

During my time in Africa, I asked the local people why they went to the witchdoctor for healing. They replied, 'There is no-one else to go to'. Many who sought healing from witchdoctors or so called 'traditional healers' were unaware of the demonic powers they may have carried. I saw many healed in Africa when the power of witchcraft was broken and the person encountered the love and power of Jesus. Witchcraft is everywhere though it is more obvious in places such as Africa. It is more hidden in Western culture in things like the occult. We can simply break its power in the Name of Jesus, and receive cleansing and healing through the powerful blood of Jesus.

Freemasonry

Many are affected by the sins and curses of their forefathers who were freemasons. This may go back generations in a family. It may also be passed from one church leader who was a freemason to the successive church leaders. Most are unaware their predecessors were linked to freemasonry since it was and still is a secret society.

There was no history of freemasonry in my family bloodline until the Lord revealed it to me on two separate occasions. The first was when I sought prayer for deliverance from a particular thing and the Lord revealed the root was freemasonry in my forefathers. The second time was when I was seeking healing, and I had a picture of a ladder, an eye and the word witchcraft. Instantly, I understood this to mean freemasonry in the bloodline.

There are many sicknesses and illnesses that are passed down the bloodline as a result of the sinful acts, curses and oaths that take place in freemasonry. Freemasonry is divided into various levels known as 'degrees'. The higher the degree means the greater the demonic power and spiritual atrocities. One of the highest degrees involves the false order of Melchizedek and it is abominable what takes place. Each degree of involvement is to be renounced and the ungodly oaths and covenants may be annulled through the blood of Jesus.

I recommend praying through some specific prayers on *Freemasonry in the Family* available from credible sources[1] [2]. This may apply to most of us, even if there is no indication of freemasonry in the family line. However, where there is indication of a higher involvement, such as 'thirty-third degree' or 'royal arch degree', then I recommend seeking the appropriate ministry that specializes in freemasonry or provides training days with in-depth prayer ministry directed at each of these degrees. [3]

I have witnessed people with pain in their neck who have been healed after receiving prayer for freemasonry. This has been especially when renouncing the 'noose around the neck' from the first degree. The first degree also includes curses spoken to the throat and tongue, and these curses may lead to a fear of choking and respiratory illnesses such as asthma or breathing difficulties.

A lady asked for prayer to break the powers of freemasonry in her family line, so we prayed through the various levels being guided through the outlined prayers. As she forgave her forefathers and renounced involvement at the different levels, her spirit responded and she felt something shift. There was another woman who was sitting in on the same session with no history of freemasonry (as far as she was aware). However, I encouraged her to participate in the prayers. As she did, her body and spirit responded to the loosing of the noose around the neck. She too was set free from demonic spirits and curses as her spirit responded to these prayers. She was so surprised by this that she looked further into her family tree, and sure enough, she discovered some of her ancestors were freemasons.

A lady asked for prayer knowing her great grandfather had been a high ranking freemason. The Holy Spirit revealed the level her grandfather had practiced, and with specific prayers for this higher degree the lady was freed from the effects of the ungodly covenants, oaths and declarations made by her great grandfather. [3]

Freemasonry is like a spider's web with an intrinsic network of curses, vows and covenants. There are various blood covenants and pacts made to Satan that we can repent of and break, and then replace with Jesus' blood of the new covenant. Jesus said His blood *is* the blood of the new covenant, which He shed for us for the forgiveness of sins. Hence, we are renewing our covenant with Jesus every time we humbly and reverently take Holy Communion.

Fetishes, Charms and 'Objects'

Before stepping on the mission field, I was very skeptical about objects carrying power. However, I have now come to the realization that objects can carry evil power. I repeatedly came across fetishes tied around people's bodies. Fetishes are pieces of string used by witchdoctors to tie around a sick part of the body (usually the neck, waist, ankles or wrists). They form a band and the band may contain knots. They are given under the false pretense that they carry power for healing. They may carry power depending on the source that they come from, though this is most likely to be demonic power. However, the person may remain sick as long as the fetish is on them. I have seen people healed the moment fetishes have been removed and their powers broken.

One of our helpers, whilst praying for a lady, sensed there was power around the lady's waist. The lady was fully clothed, but when we asked to look at her waist, a fetish was there! After removing the fetish and praying for her abdomen, she was healed.

There was a baby who was brought to me, looking quite sick. There were fetishes all over his body. I didn't find anything specific on examination. The mother agreed to have the fetishes removed and for us to pray. We broke the power of witchcraft and commanded the spirit of death to leave, and then declared life and health in Jesus' Name. A few minutes later, there was a change in the baby's appearance. The baby was happy, active and playful, and looked a normal healthy baby. Everyone agreed the baby was well and the mother laughed and smiled.

Likewise, there can be charms or objects that carry evil power. We may receive gifts that appear harmless but have evil spirits that inflict sickness or a curse. If we sense this, then it is probably best to get rid of the gift or object. Obvious objects include dragons, trolls, evil looking objects, buddha statues, crystals or objects meant to make you 'feel better'. We simply can ask the Holy Spirit if the objects or gifts are safe to have or not, no matter how much we like them or who gave them to us.

Christians who carry the healing anointing may anoint pieces of cloth to heal the sick. This was demonstrated when handkerchiefs or aprons were brought to Paul and then taken to the sick: *'God did extraordinary miracles through Paul, so that even handkerchiefs and aprons that had touched him were taken to the sick, and their illnesses were cured and the evil spirits left them,'* (Acts 19:11). I know people who have received pieces of material or cloth that carried anointing power to heal the sick. These pieces of cloth have usually had hands placed upon them by those who carry the Holy Spirit healing anointing. Those who received them may have put them on their pillow or on their body, and testified to feeling better or even healed.

A group of people acquired various jewellery after they visited a Masai Mara tribe in Kenya. They wanted to give me some necklaces they had bought from the people. When I looked at some of these necklaces, I could see and sense there was something demonic about them, making them uninviting to wear. I asked where they got them from and they said that some necklaces were made by Christians but others were from the tribal people, but they couldn't remember which were from whom. I advised them to burn the necklaces that looked uninviting. They had no idea that demonic spirits could be in objects like jewellery. As we set fire to the jewellery, an unusual huge fire came out of these small necklaces.

The Bible says that the images of other gods (and I believe this includes objects carrying demonic spirits) we are to burn. *'The images of their gods you are to burn in the fire. Do not covet the silver or gold on them and do not take it for yourselves, or you will be ensnared by it, for it is detestable to the Lord your God. Do not bring a detestable thing into your house, or you, like it, will be set apart for destruction'* (Deuteronomy 7:25-26). This warns us about bringing ungodly objects in our homes that have evil powers.

Likewise, any books on sorcery or witchcraft should be burnt and destroyed. There are so many children's books that have stories which include vampires, witches, sorcerers, dragons and demons, that seem harmless, entertaining and fun, yet their purpose is to subtly draw readers into the demonic realm and away from God. We must not be ignorant of this by falling into the deception that it is just harmless fun.

Freedom from the Occult

A list of the various occult practices has been provided (see Appendix A). Sometimes, we are not aware of the things we have opened up to, or the things our forefathers may have practiced. Praying through the list, by repenting of and then renouncing any involvement with each activity, is like a spiritual cleansing to the body, soul and spirit. Renouncing each practice is like closing the doors that we or our ancestors have opened to the occult. There is no harm, only benefits, from renouncing any possible involvement with the occult.

I would like to finish this chapter with a testimony of when I was just nineteen years old and new to deliverance ministry. I was on an outreach with Youth With A Mission as part of a Discipleship Training School, when I met a young man who had been dabbling in white witchcraft. His father, like mine, was a vicar and I saw how the enemy was drawing this young man away from God through deception. In our conversation, the Holy Spirit came on me and I gave the young man the option of choosing between the Kingdom of God and the kingdom of Satan. There and then, he suddenly asked me to pray for him before he changed his mind, as he was convicted by the truth. I looked around and all the leaders were busy ministering to other people. One leader encouraged me to pray for the man by myself. I was a bit anxious for I felt out of my depth, having never done any deliverance ministry before. However, God was in control for this was a divine appointment. After I prayed a brief prayer, I waited for a few minutes until he opened his eyes. His eyes appeared glowing and his countenance had changed, so I asked him what happened. He said he saw a bright light coming towards him and then a dark black cloak fell from his shoulders. I asked if he knew what the light was. And he said, 'Jesus!'

God is waiting to free His people even through the most inexperienced of believers. He is simply looking for willing vessels, like you and me, because He is the One who heals and sets His people free!

END NOTES:

[1] Kylstra, Chester; *Freemasonry in the Family*; Restoring The Foundations.
[2] Stevens, Selwyn; *Unmasking Freemasonry, Removing the Hoodwink*; Jubilee Publishers.
[3] Kitchen, Yvonne; *Freemasonry: Death in the Family*; Fruitful Vine Publishing House.

16

Alternative Medicines

When men tell you to consult mediums and spiritists, should not a people inquire of their God?

Isaiah 8:19

Nowadays there are a range of complementary alternative medicines that are available as other treatments for healing. My concern is the source of power that may be operating behind each alternative medicine because some may cause more harm than good with regards to healing.

Many people choose an alternative or complementary medicine in the hope of finding a cure for their symptoms. It may be that there are no medical doctors available, or there are medical doctors but they are unable to cure the problem especially if the symptoms are chronic or have spiritual and emotional roots. This chapter is to increase our awareness of the possible sources of power behind some of the alternative medicines.

Complementary Alternative Medicines

There has been an increase over the years in what is known as *Complementary and Alternative Medicines* (CAM), also known as 'holistic' or 'integrated medicines'. Most alternative medicines see health and emotional problems as a depletion or imbalance of the body's energy. Hence, their aim is to restore the flow of energy. However, it is good to find out where the source of power is coming from that restores the flow of energy, for it may be linked to spiritual roots that are potentially harmful to the spirit, soul and body.

Whereas scientifically researched medicines usually reveals the benefits and side-effects of drugs, alternative medicines don't usually reveal the potential side-effects or harm they may cause to the body, soul and spirit. This is because most are rooted in *Eastern Religions* or *Life Energy Forces*. Life energy force is known as *qi* or *chi* in China, *ki* in Japan and *prana* in India. There should be warnings about each complementary medicine in the same way we have warnings of the potential side-effects from scientifically researched drugs.

Eastern Religions & Life Energy Forces
As already mentioned, most CAM therapies have roots in eastern religion such as Taoism and Hinduism or life energy forces. This is seen, for example, in *Reflexology, Homeopathy, Reiki, Acupuncture, Chiropractice, New Age* and *Yoga*. Their aim is to tap into an energy source to release healing. Words commonly used for 'energies' are: *'yin and yang', 'chi life force', 'meridians', 'chakras', 'cosmic energy, 'universal energy', 'vital force', 'biomagnetic' and 'natural magnetism'*.

There are also medicines such as *'Naturopathy'* and *'Ayurvedic medicine'* that may give good advice on diet and lifestyle but may also have roots in eastern religion or life energy forces. In the same way we may look at the ingredients before we buy or eat a particular food, so we should look at the spiritual roots or sources of power behind each CAM before we open ourselves up to them.

External, Internal or Spiritual Treatment
CAM's may also be grouped as *external, internal* or *spiritual* treatments. Let's take a look at these.

External Treatments involve massages or manipulations. This includes *acupuncture, aromatherapy, chiropractice, osteopathy, kinesiology, reflexology, reiki* and *shiatsu*.

Internal Treatments involve fluids, oils, infusions and 'medicines' by mouth, or sometimes in the form of enemas. This includes *homeopathy, herbalism* and *naturopathy.*

Spiritual (or 'Psychic') Treatments involve *crystal therapy, transcendental meditation (TM), martial arts, faith healers (usually mediums or spiritualists), yoga* and *hypnotherapy.*

Shrewd as Snakes yet Innocent as Doves (Matthew 10:16)
Most CAM's involve a spiritual component to healing whether from life energy forces or eastern spiritualism. Many practitioners believe that 'energies' can be transmitted from one person to another. There are many Christians who are either CAM therapists or regularly receive therapy from one of these practices, under the false belief that CAM's are safe. Though the CAM's may appear good and the people practicing them say they are Christians or even doctors, I believe in most cases the source of power is not from God. As a Christ follower and a doctor, I believe we are to seek Christ for our healing, or go through natural resources that God has provided, and scientific research has proven to be medically beneficial to our health.

Paul said to test everything and hold on to good but avoid all kinds of evil (1 Thessalonians 5:21-22). The only source of power which is guaranteed to be safe is the power of the Holy Spirit. *'Do not turn to mediums or seek out spiritists for* **you will be defiled by them.** *I am the Lord your God'* (Leviticus 19:31). *'When men tell you to consult mediums and spiritists, who whisper and mutter, should not a people* **inquire of their God**' (Isaiah 8:19). I believe this applies to the sources of healing offered today. Instead of believing what others may say, we are to inquire of the Lord.

If we are seekers of the truth then it is good to seek His Spirit for guidance before seeking an alternative therapy. I have seen people being set free from the spirits behind acupuncture, homeopathy, reiki, reflexology and yoga ... to name just some.

A lady came to me with pain in her lower back and happened to lead yoga classes. Her back pain started after she began the classes. She was a church-going Christian, yet seemed to be unaware of the eastern spirits linked to yoga. When I mentioned the *kundalini spirit* in yoga and how it can reside in the lower back, she asked for some prayer. After she confessed and renounced the kundalini spirit, her back pain immediately disappeared and she was healed. However, she chose to continue her classes and the pain returned. I bumped into her a second time, and graciously explained that she was to give up the practice if she wanted to stay healed.

There was a visiting missionary who brought a team of volunteers to our base in Mozambique. She was apparently in the healing ministry and openly shared how she practiced homeopathy, reflexology, acupuncture and many other CAM's. It had become her family business and source of income. She had a desire to heal the sick but had come under deception that these practices were good and acceptable to God, since she had inherited them from her mother. At first, she couldn't accept how the source of power wasn't from God. So I prayed and asked God to open her eyes to the truth. She went away to pray and soon returned with fresh conviction from the Holy Spirit. She came out with a huge list of alternative practices she had been involved in over the years, and chose to lay them all down and never pick them up again. So she repented, forgave her Mum for introducing her to them, and renounced the spirits behind each one. After this, there was a change in her facial countenance. At first she looked dazed but commented how something amazing had happened. It was as if a reset button had been pressed as the veil of deception was lifted from her eyes. Her face and eyes looked different as they shone with the radiance of Christ. She chose from now on to rely on the power of the Holy Spirit for healing others. I advised her to get rid of her books. As her eyes were opened to the truth, she couldn't believe the deception she had been under all these years. *'Many of those who believed now came and confessed their evil deeds. A number who had practiced sorcery, brought their scrolls together and burned them publicly'* (Acts 19:18).

I was teaching and ministering healing in Mozambique when a Brazilian doctor witnessed what I was doing. He approached me and was interested in the 'power' I used to heal the sick, for he noticed the people recovered after prayer. I was reminded of Simon the sorcerer who asked Peter for the power he used to heal the sick (Acts 8:18-20). As we chatted, I could see he wanted to heal the sick, but had been accessing powers from 'alternative' sources. He had been involved in Hinduism, Buddhism, reiki, homeopathy, yoga, acupuncture, and nearly every alternative medicine. I could see a heaviness and darkness in his eyes as he realized he had made the wrong choices by seeking the wrong powers. I explained how the power came from the Holy Spirit, as a result of having a relationship with God. If he wanted it, he could have it, but only if he was willing to repent and turn from his ungodly sources of power and choose to pursue a relationship with Jesus. I asked him if he wanted to be free of the spirits he had partnered with over the years through the various alternative practices. He did and willingly renounced each one, and then invited Jesus into his heart. I prayed for him and his countenance changed. The heaviness lifted and his eyes appeared lighter. He felt a peace in his inner being, and I encouraged him to pursue Jesus from now on.

Commonly Available Alternative Medicines

This last section provides a very brief overview and summary of the commonly available alternative medicines, highlighting the source of power used in the various therapies. I am no expert in this field and I am very aware there may be differing facts and opinions with regards to these practices. Not all therapies have been listed, so please check out the alternative practices not mentioned here. If anyone has been involved in complementary alternative medicines, I suggest you enquire of the Lord if this alternative practice is acceptable to Him. And if not, then we can simply repent and renounce the life energy forces or eastern spirits involved with each practice, and ask Jesus to cleanse our whole being (body, soul and spirit) with His blood. I believe it is better to be cleansed and set free, rather than remain in bondage through deception.

Reiki

What is it? 'Reiki' is a Japanese word and was apparently founded by a Japanese Buddhist monk. It is formed from two parts: *'Rei'* meaning wisdom and knowledge of all the universe, and *'Ki'* meaning life force energy. Simply put, 'Rei' means **'universal'** & 'Ki' means **'life force'**. It has been linked to Hinduism, Yoga and other spiritual channels.

What is the Spiritual Root? Reiki energy comes from the 'Higher Power' or universal life force. It uses auras, chakras, meridians and dowsing to transfer universal life force energy to other people. It is believed each person has seven chakras or areas of receptivity inside, from which the emotion and healing is expressed. Meridians are pathways to the chakras.

What does it do? Everyone is believed to have a field of energy or 'aura' surrounding them. By the 'laying on of hands' the energy or power channels through the practitioner's body are transferred to the body of the person receiving the healing.

Reiki is not to be confused with the laying on of hands, as described in the book of Acts (Acts 8:17). This is because Reiki's source of power is not the Holy Spirit. It may provide some short term improvement but equally may cause long term issues.

How is it received? The practitioner is an open channel for the life force to flow through them and out of their hands to the patient. A person becomes a practitioner through paying for a Reiki seminar, and opening up spiritually to the Reiki rituals of the Reiki master. After this, the Reiki energy starts flowing automatically whenever the person places their hands on somebody, thus channelling the Reiki energy through themself to the other person. The practitioner receives the life energy force whilst giving it to others as a 'protection' and a 'blessing'. Apparently, after daily self-treatments with Reiki, "further spiritual growth" and an increasing addiction to Reiki is guaranteed. There is a second level where Reiki power is sent over a distance to another person. The highest level is becoming a Reiki master.

This is obviously a counterfeit source of healing that mimics the way the Holy Spirit heals the sick through the laying on of hands. We can't buy the Holy Spirit. It is freely given by God to His children. This was seen with Simon the sorcerer when he offered Peter money to buy the power from the Holy Spirit to use in his practice. Peter replied: *'May your money perish with you, because you thought you could buy the gift of God with money! You have no part or share in this ministry, because your heart is not right before God'* (Acts 8:20-22).

Yoga

What is it? Yoga means to be 'yoked' and is a path for dissociating the conscious level of the mind. It is an eastern meditation which involves being yoked to Hindu gods (Shiva, Brahma, and others) or becoming united with the cosmic spirits. There is no innocent form of yoga or such a thing as 'Christian yoga'! I believe this is a false label.

What is the Spiritual Root? The spiritual root is eastern spiritism rooted in Hinduism. It is new age and associated with chanting of mantras.

What does it do? Many think yoga is a good form of exercise, relaxation and stretching. The purpose of Yoga, as taught by Hindu teachers, is to unite the human spirit to Hindu gods by various physical postures. Hence, physical exercise can't be separated from spiritual involvement. It is a form of Hindu worship. Its goal is self-realisation of one's personal divinity or god consciousness and awakens the ***kundilini*** spirit. The *kundilini* spirit is a snake which coils at the base of the spine and causes lower back pain. Kundalini is the 'enlightenment' that the practice of Yoga is designed to 'awaken'.

How is it Received? Many of the postures in yoga are linked to the Hindu deity. There are four types of Yoga (see other sources for further information on these). The western yoga is based on the 'Hatha' yoga, which is a subdivision of the Raja type. This is the way of contemplation and meditation.

When a person takes on Yoga they may come under the kundilini spirit and this can cause lower back pain.

Reflexology

What is it? Reflexology, also called 'zone therapy' or 'compression massage', is a technique which involves the massaging of one's feet at specific points to bring relaxation or relief of pain in another part of the body. There are usually ten 'energy lines' that are meant to run longitudinally through the body, five to each foot linking all organs along these lines. Controlled pressure is applied to each reflex point on the foot. For example, by massaging the big toe in the appropriate places, you can ease head pains, thyroid, and neck problems. Each part of the body is represented by a specific reflex area, usually on the foot. Reflexology, however, is not limited to the feet. The hands or ears are said to contain these same points, or "zones." It is similar to acupuncture.

What does it do? It is used to relieve pain in the body. Described as a holistic therapy, reflexology aims to benefit the body, mind, emotions and spirit. It is said to work by unblocking 'energy channels' running up from the foot to an organ affected by malfunction or disease, allowing the free flow of 'life energy' necessary for healing and good health.

What are the Spiritual Roots? It is rooted in life energy forces which flow through these zones or meridians, also known as energy channels, to reflex points in the feet. They are divided into one of two energy forces known in the Orient, as yin and yang. Yin and yang are considered to be opposites. Yin represents the night, dark, feminine, left side of the body, eternity, etc. Yang is its opposite and represents day, light, masculine, right side of the body, history, etc. In fact, many Christians who practice reflexology are most likely to be unaware of what is really behind reflexology's "respectable" front.

How is it Received? The feet are palpated lightly, noting particularly any areas of tenderness or 'grittiness'. Experienced therapists claim to be able to identify organs which are suffering from an imbalance of vital energy and the channels which need to be unblocked to bring about healing. A general massage of the foot, during which the patient is encouraged to relax, is followed by detailed massage of reflex points whilst holding the foot in specific grips. Finger techniques involve pressure, rotation, and finger and thumb 'walking' across the foot. Although these are thought to be less effective, similar techniques may also be used on the hands.

Life energy forces and eastern spirits appear to be the sources of power in this practice.

Acupuncture

What is it? Acupunture is a traditional form of Chinese medicine which involves stimulating the skin at strategic places, called *acupuncture points*. The first explanation for acupuncture came out of Chinese culture and belief that there are two opposing life forces (*Yin* and *Yang*) which circulate in twelve special channels (known as meridians) throughout the body. However, a modern acupuncturist may not use or believe in the meridians and use their own acupuncture points. It is similar to reflexology but uses needles instead of massaging the skin.

What does it do? It believes that disease is caused by an imbalance of the Yin and Yang forces and can be rectified by regulating the flow of energy in these meridians. This can be achieved by stimulating acupuncture points located along these meridians, through fine needles inserted in the skin. It may also use laser, heat or electricity to do this. Nowadays, it may be used as an anaesthetic, a preventative or to relieve symptoms.

What are the Spiritual Roots? It originates from the beliefs of Taoism. These beliefs are that there are yin-yang forces which flow along invisible pathways in the body called meridians, and illness results from an imbalance in these forces, or the blockage of these forces. Hence, spiritual energy or life forces are used to bring equilibrium to the body and restore health.

How is it Received? It is received by inserting needles, lasers, heat or electricity at certain points, and this is supposed to allow a balanced flow of the body's yin and yang energies.

There are theories that acupuncture works, either because the placement of the needles sends signals to the brain which release endorphins, or because the needles block a pain signal to the brain. However, these theories have not been proven. Even if these theories prove correct, acupuncture is based on the idea that relief is coming from the flowing of chi and balancing of yin and yang.

Traditional Herbalists

What is it? Herbalism or herbal medicine is an alternative medical therapy defined as the use of plants or substances derived from plants to help treat disease. Before the application of science based medicines, traditional medicines were mostly herbal. Though herbal medicines may be safe and effective, *some* herbal remedies may consist of harmful toxic substances that cause serious illness or death, especially when used in excess amounts.

What are the Spiritual Roots? Whilst plants in themselves have no specific spiritual influence, the spiritual beliefs or practices of the practitioner (particularly Traditional Chinese Medicine, Ayurvedic Medicine and New Age therapists or witch doctors and shamanists) may be harmful.

Traditional Chinese Herbal Medicine is based on Taoism and the principle of balancing chi, the universal life force or energy. Ayurvedic Indian medicine has strong Hindu associations involving chakras (energy centres). Traditional medicine practiced in Africa is commonly done by Shamans or witchdoctors and linked to spiritism.

What does it do? There are many medical benefits from plants and herbs, but the problems are either from incorrect doses or from the person who gives it. Since the doses aren't scientifically tested, there is a danger of giving too much or too little. Herbal remedies may contain unknown substances or even be contaminated, since they are not scientifically tested. Also, too much may cause toxic side-effects and too little may lead to the development of drug-resistance.

Many herbal medicines are being used for treating various ailments. An example is the treatment with *Artemisia annua,* given as a Chinese herbal drink in the prevention of malaria. From this Chinese plant, artemisinin based drugs have been scientifically tested and produced in optimum doses for the treatment of malaria. The problem is the emerging of drug-resistance from taking the herbal drink in suboptimal doses on a regular basis for the prevention of malaria. The artemisinin given as a herbal drink will initially be effective in preventing malaria, until the parasites become resistant to the sub-optimal doses. When the individual develops malaria, the scientifically tested drug doses of artemisinin will no longer work, because the malaria parasites have developed a resistance to this particular drug. Instead, another drug will be required to treat the malaria parasites.

Some missionaries bought a bag of the *artemisia annua* herbal drink and took it on a daily basis for many months. They believed it prevented them getting malaria, and were probably right. However, one day they tested positive for malaria symptoms, so they took the artemesinin-based medical tablets, but the tablets had no effect because the parasites had now become resistant to this drug. An alternative drug was available to treat the malaria.

How is it Received? Some herbal medicines are given orally or in the form of a drink. Others may be put on the skin or wound in the form of a paste. Some are given to wear around the sick part of the body. This is known as a fetish when given by shamanists or witchdoctors.

Many herbal medicines are good and cause no harm, though some may cause more harm than good.

Aromatherapy

What is it? Aromatherapy is the use of essential oils from aromatic plants. The oils are diluted and used either in baths, as vapours or massaged in the skin.

What does it do? The oils are meant to keep the person balanced both emotionally and physically. The oils may be toxic to the body when used incorrectly or absorbed via the skin into the blood. However, most vapours from the oils stimulate a relaxed response.

What are the Spiritual Roots? It dates back to 3,500 BC where ancient Egyptians were seen using aromatic substances in medicine. Modern day French men developed the therapy and stated there were electrical charges in the essential oils that helped bring about healing. Some therapists may use 'spiritual powers' through laying on of hands or pendulum swinging or life forces or aura detection, where they 'spiritually sense' which essential oil to give.

How is it Received? It is received over the counter or through a therapist. It can be given in drops, via inhalation, capsules or massage therapy.

Again, wisdom and discernment is required to know the source of the essential oil and the source of power linked to the person who is giving it.

Homeopathy

What is it? Samuel Hahnemann, the founder, was a freemason and follower of Confucius. Homeopathy derives from two Greek words, *homoios* meaning 'like', and *patheia* meaning 'pain or suffering'. The Oxford Dictionary defines it as: *'the treatment of disease by minute doses of drugs that in healthy persons would produce symptoms like those of the disease'*.

What does it do? It is meant to treat *'like curing like'*, through using a minute, insignificant form of one particle of the disease. However, this dosage is not possible to treat a sickness. Even vaccines require a significant dose to stimulate a response in the immune system. It is based on the greater the dilution, the greater is the effect or 'potentization'. This is done through successive vigorous shakings, known as *'succussion'*.

What are the Spiritual Roots? A life energy force is imparted in the shaking between successive dilutions. There is no scientific proof it can have any more effect than a placebo, since there is negligible dosage. Hence, this proves there is a 'universal power' imparted through shaking.

How is it Received? It is given by mouth as a liquid or pill.

Homeopathy is clearly linked to a life energy force, where the power is imparted through the 'shaking' by the person who is producing the 'medicines'.

Chiropractice

What is it? The word 'chiro' is from the Greek word meaning 'hands,' and 'practer' from the Greek meaning 'practice'. It is manual treatment with the hands on the muscles, bones and joints, especially the back.

What does it do? It is meant to heal through manipulation by releasing a flow of energy in the body. Scientific studies have shown it has no significant effect or change on the body and may cause harm in the process.

What are the Spiritual Roots? It was founded by Palmer, who was into magnetic healing and hypnosis. He believed the 'flow of innate intelligence' through the body is linked to the 'universal life energy force', and by releasing this flow through manipulation of the spinal column, healing could take place.

How is it received? It is received by manipulating the bones, muscles or joints back into place.

The healing may be from life energy forces used by the chiropractors, and I encourage each believer to enquire of the Lord if it is safe to see a chiropractor before they do.

Osteopathy

What is it? Osteopathy is physical manipulation of 'osteopathic' areas in the spine. Through 'intuitive' palpation on the skin, osteopathic areas are detected. Osteopathic lesions are not clinically or radiologically proven to be valid.

What does it do? This spiritual sensing followed by physical manipulation is meant to bring about self-healing, either to the spine or elsewhere in the body. The manipulation may cause stiffness, soreness, headache and tiredness.

What are the Spiritual Roots? It is referred to as being 'holistic' with spiritual connections to the 'divine intelligence' or 'grand architect of the universe'. Since 'sensing' the osteopathic areas is described as a main feature, the source or power behind this is spiritualism.

How is it Received? It is received by palpating the spine and then applying manipulation at the 'osteopathic' areas.

Again, osteopathy sounds a natural way of treatment but may involve using power from other sources.

Hypnosis

What is it? *'Hypnos'* is the Greek god of 'sleep'. It is a trance or altered state of consciousness, induced by repeating a word or by concentrating on a rhythmical object moving back and forth.

What does it do? In the hypnotic state, the mind of the patient is under the will or control of the hypnotist. Self-will or self-control is lost during the session. (Self-control is a fruit of the Spirit, whereas being controlled or manipulated by someone is a form of witchcraft). The danger is allowing the mind to be influenced by other powers or sources. People who receive therapy may later develop mental health issues, such as, oppression, torment, personality changes, possession by spirits and the feeling of being manipulated.

What are the Spiritual Roots? Forms of hypnosis have been used in Shamans, medicine men and ancient priests who use such techniques along with their 'spiritual' powers. It may be used in modern day psychiatric practice. The dangers come from opening up the mind to possible demonic sources through the loss of self-control.

How is it Received? It is received when a person is willing to let another person have control of their mind, as they voluntarily let go of their conscious state.

We are to be wise with regards to losing our self-control or submitting the control of our mind (conscious, subconscious and unconscious) to another person or spirit. The safe and trustworthy person to whom we may surrender our body, soul and spirit, (especially our mind, will and emotions) is Jesus, Father God and the Holy Spirit.

Anaesthetic drugs behave in a different way for their purpose is to sedate a person during a surgical procedure. Anesthetic drugs are scientifically researched and tested, and the anaesthetist will inform the patient of the benefits as well as the possible side effects of the medicine.

Martial Arts

I have included martial arts in the list (though it probably isn't recognized as a CAM), because it may be used to improve mental awareness and is a form of stress management. Some use it for gaining greater power. The common martial arts include: *Jiu Jitsu, Karate, Taekwondo, Tai Chi, Judo and Kick Boxing.*

What is it? Martial arts are based on self-defence, relaxation, increase in mental awareness, and increase in physical power. Each martial art can connect a person to demonic spirits, for the physical powers can't be separated from the spiritual powers. It is the belief that man has the power within himself to be superhuman or 'godlike'. This is a form of power-control. Satan fell from God's Kingdom because he wanted to be like God; *'I will ascend above the tops of the clouds; I will make myself like the Most High'* (Isaiah 14:14).

What does it do? As the student progresses in the control of his/her motor skills and balance, they are slowly introduced to the idea and principles of breath control and "internal" strength or power. According to eastern mysticism, breathing is both a physical and spiritual exercise. The ability to control ones breathing and respiration is used to enter an **altered state of consciousness**, or 'hypnosis'. This then opens the door from the physical to the spirit world. Deep breathing and meditation are then presented to enhance one's physical abilities. This is often being taught as a new form of 'science' or 'metaphysics.' It is a potent mixture of ancient occult practices with scientific terminology attached. The masters of kung-fu teach that chi is like the batteries inside the toy. Chi is what creates real power. At black belt level, most often, "internal" or "chi" training is used in the demonstration of breaking boards or bricks. This can cause a spirit of 'mind-block' which prevents a person from hearing God or connecting with God's Spirit.

What are the Spiritual Roots? Martial arts are usually rooted in false religions or false gods. In many cases, there may be covenants made with the spirit of death. What they teach, known as "god" by the western Christian world, is actually an energy force, or "great spirit", and that through proper breathing techniques, meditation, mantras, spiritual exercises and life style, we may all become one with this 'divine energy.'

How is it Received? It is received by attending classes and following the leader with an open spirit.

There are testimonies from people who have been involved in martial arts and reached black belt or leadership level, who warned others of the spiritual bondage and demonic powers involved. It is full of deception behind the temptation to gain power. The power is from demonic spirits that may take over and possess an individual. The spirits may cause mind-block, and this prevents a person from hearing God. Such are the testimonies of those who have been delivered and set free, and now minister under the power of the Holy Spirit.[1]

Response to Alternative Medicines

Most alternative medicines, as described above, may be under the influence of ungodly sources. Anyone who has been involved in such practices may renounce the influence of eastern spirits or life energy forces, and renounce the universal powers and ungodly spirits behind such powers. Where there are spirits linked to a practice, then these can be addressed and renounced (such as the *kundalini spirit* in Yoga, *Yin and Yang* in reflexology and acupuncture, spirit of mind-block and covenant with death as seen in martial arts). If alternative medicines have been practiced in the family, then the blood-line can also be cleansed. Once the spiritual power behind an alternative medicine has been renounced, then the spiritual door is to remain closed by the individual choosing not to return to the practice.

This is a simple overview to help the reader become more aware of the complementary alternative medicines that are widely available today, and to help encourage everyone to seek further information including the truth behind each CAM. The most important thing is to enquire of the Lord about the 'source of power' or 'spiritual root' that is behind each person or practice, and if it is acceptable to Him or not.

May the Lord guide us with His Spirit of truth and discernment, so we may discern what is acceptable and pleasing to Him and what to avoid.

END-NOTES

[1] Mantofa, Philip; *Warrior For Revival; (Destiny Image, 2011)*

HEALING TOOLS

17

Prophetic Blessings

They will put My Name on the Israelites and I will bless them

Numbers 6:27

A healing tool that may be used at the end of a ministry session is a prophetic blessing. This is where the facilitator or minister prays a blessing for the participant. It becomes prophetic when we speak from the heart of God to the heart of a person.

I first heard about the power of a blessing from Roy Godwin[1], the former executive director of the Ffald-y-Brenin retreat centre in Wales. I attended a meeting where Roy shared various testimonies about people being hit by the power of God and giving their lives to Jesus after they received a blessing. Every visitor at the retreat centre in Wales would receive a blessing but this would be very different to the blessings we are familiar with. The blessings spoken at the retreat centre carried power because the member of staff who said the blessing would pray from the heart of God.

Blessings are powerful when they are ministered from the heart of God. Most people may casually say 'God bless you' but few may release words from the heart of God in the form of a prayer. A blessing is a spiritual weapon. Jesus taught us to bless our enemies instead of curse them because there is more power when we choose to bless instead of curse.

Another thing about a blessing is it is an amazing tool to release healing and freedom when reaching out to non-Christians and ministering to people in the marketplace. It is interesting that some people may not want prayer, but will gladly accept a blessing, because people like blessings. A prophetic blessing is a form of prayer as we declare God's will and purpose over a person's life. For example, we can bless a person to bear much fruit, know all truth, receive peace, and overcome their battles.

A blessing is released when we pray a blessing *in the name of Jesus* because He is the one who blesses and not us. The prayer may start with these words: *'I bless you, in the Name of Jesus, to...'* or *'May the Lord bless you to...'* This can be followed by saying things such as, *'... to know all truth and bear much fruit in your life. May He bless your relationships and bring unity in the family. May you encounter His love in a real way and know freedom in your heart from all fears, anxieties and stress. May He bless your health and finances, and may you encounter His peace...'* It is powerful when we pray for people to know the truth because Jesus is the source of all truth, so in effect we are praying they will know Him. And when we bless the person to bear fruit, we are referring to Kingdom fruit which comes from a relationship with God. Likewise, when we bless a person to encounter peace we are praying they will encounter Jesus for He is the Prince of peace.

There was a lady in my church who I didn't know very well and one Sunday when we were praying for one another I decided to offer her a prophetic blessing. I blessed her in the name of Jesus with things I sensed God wanted me to declare over her life, such as being the head and not the tail and to know God's love in a deeper way. I blessed her family to be at peace with one another, along with other things. Tears flowed down her face as I said this blessing. She thanked me so much and her husband said the prayer was spot on and powerful. I believe we can all pray prophetic blessings as we feel God's heart for His people and declare His goodness in their lives including restoring their health and relationships.

One day, as I was reaching out to people in my local town, I noticed a security guard taking a break. So I said 'Hello' and got chatting to him. He said he was a pagan and didn't want any prayer. However, when I asked if he would like a blessing, he accepted. As I looked into his eyes, I sensed he was lonely and there was rejection. So I blessed him in the name of Jesus to have good relationships and for him to have peace and joy in his life. I continued to bless him as I felt God's heart for him. At the end of the blessing he smiled with watery eyes and thanked me, so I gave him a hug. I felt God's love for him and this was released through a prophetic blessing.

The Lord instructed Aaron to release a priestly blessing on the Israelites. This well known prayer has become known as the Aaronic prayer or priestly blessing, and is usually said by the priest at the end of a service:

'The Lord bless you and keep you; the Lord make His face shine upon you and be gracious to you; the Lord turn His face toward you and give you His peace'. However, God finishes by saying: *'So they will put My Name on the Israelites and I will bless them'* (Numbers 6:22-27). When we pray a blessing in the *Name of Jesus*, then He will bless it. It is the Lord who blesses and not us.

A blessing may be said at the end of a ministry session, where the minister prays a blessing for the person who has received the healing. For example, where the person may have dealt with self-hate and rejection, then the person can be blessed to walk in wholeness and freedom and draw closer to the heart of God as they discover their true identity as a son/daughter of the King....and so on. This can be a powerful and beautiful way to end a session, as the blessing is released from the heart of God.

Prophetic blessings may be released over people, churches, shops, businesses, and neighbourhoods. It is an excellent tool for ministering healing in the market place or reaching out to non-Christians because in the majority of cases no-one will refuse a blessing. Blessings are powerful and something we can do in everyday life to help release God's love to those around us.

END NOTES

[1] Roy Godwin: *The Way of Blessing; (CPI group UK, 2016)*

HEALING TOOLS

CONCLUSION

Healing tools are divine keys to unlock various areas in the heart to release healing and freedom. However, to use these tools effectively requires pursuing an intimate relationship with God. From personal experience I have witnessed healing flow in greater power and measure when I've ministered in the Presence of God.

Over the years, I have learnt to step back and welcome the Holy Spirit into a healing session. My role is to assist Him by welcoming His Presence so He may minister in the deep areas of people's hearts. Many times we may get it wrong because we judge based on what we think or see with the flesh. Far more may be accomplished when we surrender to the Holy Spirit because He ministers far better than we can. Not only that, but we learn through seeing what He does in each given situation.

Having the appropriate tools enables us to minister in specific areas, such as *forgiveness, cleansing from generational sins, breaking soul-ties, vows, curses, covenants,* and so forth. As we yield to His Spirit and become more sensitive to hear Him, the easier it will become to minister alongside Him.

Volume Two has provided a range of healing tools that are available and these tools will prepare the reader for Volume Three, *Divine Heart Surgery.* In the same way a General Surgeon requires the necessary skills and experiences before he or she may specialize in heart surgery, so the same applies to us. First, the Lord will train us in the basic and general areas of healing, before He leads us to assist Him in the more specialized areas of ministry. In order to assist Him, our hearts are to be in rhythm with His heartbeat, and this develops from a life of abiding in His Presence.

God is looking for ordinary people, like you and me, to heal the sick, set the captives free, and bind up the broken-hearted, as we choose to co-labour with our Great Physician, Jesus.

RECOMMENDED FURTHER READING

Arthur Burk: *Blessing Your Spirit*
Dr Caroline Leaf: *Who Switched off my Brain*
Benny Hinn: *The Blood*
Mahesh Chavda: *The Hidden Power of the Blood of Jesus*
Wendy Alec: *Visions from Heaven*
Heidi Baker: *Birthing the Miraculous*
Joyce Meyer: *The Battle Belongs to the Lord*
Chester Kylstra: *Biblical Healing & Deliverance*
Dawna Desilva &Teresa Liebscher: *Sozo*
Dawna Desilva &Teresa Liebscher: *Basic/Advanced Sozo Manuals*
Bill Johnson & Randy Clark: *Essential Guide to Healing*
Mark Virkler: *How to Hear God's Voice*
Tony Stoltzfus: *The Calling Journey*
Henry Wright: *A More Excellent Way*
T.L Osborn: *Healing the Sick*
James Goll: *The Lost Art of Practicing His Presence*
Ana Mendez-Ferrell: *Regions of Captivity*
John Eckhardt: *Deliverance and Spiritual Warfare*
Bill Johnson: *Supernatural Power of a Transformed Mind*
John & Mark Sandford: *Deliverance and Inner Healing*
John & Paula Sandford: *Healing the Wounded Spirit*
Neil Anderson: *The Bondage Breaker*
Neil Anderson: *Freedom In Christ*
Pablo Bottari: *Free in Christ*
Jim Banks: *The Effects of Trauma*
Joan Hunter: *Freedom Beyond Comprehension*
Roberts Liardon: *John G Lake on Healing*
Roberts Liardon: *God's Generals- The Healing Evangelists*
Roberts Liardon: *Breaking Controlling Powers*
Morris Cerullo: *Demolishing Demonic Strongholds*
Dr David Stevens: *Jesus M.D*
Don Basham: *Deliver Us From Evil*
A.W Tozer: *Pursuit of God*
Kathy Oates: *Open My Heart, Lord*
Mahesh Chavda: *Hidden Power of Prayer and Fasting*

Mark Nysewander: *The Fasting Key*
Kathie Walters: *Spirit of False Judgement*
Francis Macnutt: *Healing*
John Paul Jackson: *Art of Hearing God*
Richard Ing: *Waging Spiritual Warfare*
Randy Clark: *Power, Holiness & Evangelism*
Julia Loren: *Supernatural Anointing*
Yvonne Kitchen: *Freemasonry; Death in the Family*
Bill Radmall: *Insight into Addiction*
Roy Godwin: *The Way of Blessing*
Robert Henderson: *Operating in the Courts of Heaven*
Robert Henderson: *Healing in the Courts of Heaven*

Appendix A: List of the Occult

Here is a list of some of the occult practices. The list is not a complete list but acts as a guide, and can be used as a reference for cleansing the bloodlines from these sins with the power of the blood of Jesus (that is, after repentance, receiving forgiveness and renouncing each practice).

African occult spirits	Incantations
Animal spirits	Levitations
Antichrist spirit	Mediums
Astral projection	Mental telepathy
Astrology	Necromancy
Automatic writing	Occult & witchcraft books
Behemoth	Ouija board
Black magic	Pagan temples
Child Sacrifice	Palm reading
Clairvoyance	Pendulum
Conjuration	Psychic healing/ reading
Crystal ball	Reading tea leaves
Death & Suicide	Reincarnation
Demon worship	Satanic worship
Dispatching demons	Seances
Dowsing	Sorcery/ spells
Divination	Spiritism/ spirit guide
Eastern meditation	Table tipping
Eight ball	Tarot cards
ESP	Third eye
Evil eye	Transcendental Meditation
Faith healers	Trance
False gifts & false tongues	Vampire
Fortune telling	Voodoo
Heavy Metal	Water witching/ water spirits
Hexing (spells)	Werewolf
Homeopathy	White magic
Horoscopes	Wicca/ Witchcraft
Horror movies	
Hypnosis	
I-Ching	

Appendix B: Generational Sins & Curses

Here is a list of Generational Sins and this can be modified according to each culture. It is by no means a complete list but acts as a guide. Each section can be confessed aloud, either individually or in a group. We can then claim our inheritance as children of God.

REPENTANCE: *'I now confess the sins in my father's and mother's blood line all the way back to the fourth generation. I confess and repent of....'* (The person may either go through the whole list or make it easier by splitting the list into subgroups)

a) WITCHCRAFT & EVIL POWER- I repent of satanism, witchcraft, occult power, divination, sorcery, hearing evil voices, jezebel spirit/control, leviathan spirit, fetishes, levitation, drinking blood & cannibalism, python spirit and divination.
b) ALTAR SACRIFICES- I repent of sacrifices made to ancestors or other spirits, pagan worship, worshipping the dead, worshiping trees, animals, snakes, water spirits, worshipping rain, fear of spirits, or any other idolatry. Sexual rituals & ungodly rituals. Demonic contracts or covenants made through blood sacrifices (including babies) on altars. Demonic power bought with blood sacrifices (animal or humans).
c) OCCULT- I repent of involvement with mediums, psychics, witchdoctors, fortune-teller, necromancer, tea-leaves, palm reading, water witching, astrology, mind-control, divination, and familiar spirits (any others?)...
d) RELIGION- I repent of spirit of antichrist, religious spirit, disunity, law & duty, punishment & judgement, muslim spirit, traditionalism, unforgiveness, spiritual pride, unhealthy fear of God, secret societies, freemasons - setting up system of Babylon, altar sacrifices, illegal trading
e) TRAUMA- I repent of war spirit, killing the innocent, effects of war (physical & mental), fear, death, unresolved grief, torture, rape, violence, loss, imprisonment
f) TRIBALISM– I repent of war spirit & Nimrod spirit (power & control with rulership & destructive spirit), torture. Pride in clan and tribe to kill, steal or destroy others. Blood altars for power of land and over people.
g) WARS-- I repent of using demonic contracts to gain power, voting for evil governments, superiority over another tribe, killing people to gain power/rulership

HEALING TOOLS

h) SLAVERY- I repent of child slavery, sex trafficking, trade routes from nation to nation across waters, selling children for money
i) ILLEGAL TRADING- I repent of corruption with money, putting people in slavery to enrich self, underpaid workers, bribery to get what want, misuse of money, stolen goods or cheating others, avoiding tax, using government money for self gain, illegal documents (fake, counterfeit),illegal businesses eg- money from brothels, black market, drug dealing
j) REBELLION- I repent of independent spirit, unsubmissive, lying, resistance, disobedience, covenants with death, witchcraft, stiff neck
k) DOMINATION- I repent of control, manipulation, possessiveness, male domination & female slavery, other cultural beliefs (state them-), mocking
l) PRIDE - I repent of racism, false humility, vanity, self-importance, cultural superiority, respect & reputation, self-righteousness
m) CHRONIC FINANCIAL PROBLEMS- I repent of possessiveness with money, job losses, poverty spirit, stealing, debt, spirit of mammon, illegal trading
n) INFERIORITY- I repent of intimidation, self-hate, self-condemnation, insecurity, shame, not good enough, low self-worth, victim mindset
o) REJECTION- I repent of abandonment, insecurity, victimization, absent father, absent mother, orphan spirit, not wanted, self-pity, fear of rejection
p) PERFORMANCE- I repent of envy, jealousy, competitive, striving, people pleasing, feeling of inadequacy, low self esteem, seeking approval & recognition, operating out of soul instead of spirit (lust for power, opinions, self-will, decisions, tradition, judging according to culture)
q) SEXUAL SINS - I repent of adultery, abuse, incest, lust, rape, pornography, fornication (any others?)...
r) PREMATURE DEATHS- I repent of attempted suicide, murder, abortions, premature death, killing the innocent, divorce, spirit of death.
s) GUILT- I repent of false guilt, blame & shame, self-hate, embarrassment, disgrace, defilement, failure
t) ADDICTION - I repent of alcohol, smoking, drugs, sex, pornography, food (anything else?)...
u) HEREDITARY ILLNESSES- I repent of sicknesses, allergies, heart problems, disabilities, cancers, chronic sickness, migraines, blood diseases, epilepsy, barrenness (due to sexual sin), and also?

v) MENTAL health- I repent of depression, anxiety, fears, panic attacks, compulsive obsessions, suicide, confusion, craziness, distraction, schizophrenia, agreement with death, epilepsy, learning problems..
w) NEGATIVE ATTITUDE - I repent of anger, hatred to women (or men), revenge, violence, bitterness, judging & criticism, condemning, unforgiveness, deception, lies, rebellion, pride, stubbornness, control & manipulation, unbelief, mistrust, double-mindedness, division, complaining, accusing others, self-pity
x) FEARS- I repent of intimidation, fear of man, sickness, death, being attacked, demons, authorities, violence (or any other known fears)...

RECEIVE FORGIVENESS & FORGIVE: *'Lord, I forgive my parents, grandparents, and forefathers for these sins and ungodly inheritances which have come on me. Lord Jesus, I ask you to forgive me and my forefathers, through the power of Your blood.'* (take time to receive His forgiveness in your heart).

RENOUNCE SINS & BREAK CURSES & COVENANTS: *'I now renounce these generational sins and break all curses attached to the sins in the powerful Name of Jesus. May they no longer have an influence on me or my children'*

'Lord, I ask You to break all ungodly covenants in my mother's and father's line in the Name of Jesus.' (This applies to covenants with demonic spirits through ungodly trade deals, worshipping ancestral spirits, pacts with witchdoctors or secret societies, or as the Holy Spirit reveals. Name the ungodly covenants or trade deals and ask Jesus to annul them through the power of His blood - Is 28:18.)

RECEIVE CLEANSING: *'Lord, I ask You to cleanse my father's and mother's bloodline all the way back to the fourth generation, as it says in Your Word, for all these confessed sins. Cleanse and heal my body, soul and spirit through the power of Your blood. I receive by faith, the healing and freedom from all demonic influences, in Jesus' mighty name. Thank you for cleansing me and setting me free'.* (Take time to thank and praise Him).

REPLACE with BLESSINGS: *'Lord, I ask You to bless me and my children with Your Kingdom DNA and Kingdom inheritance as a child of God, in Jesus' Name. Thank you Jesus.'* (You can be specific by declaring blessings on the areas confessed, such as, blessings on health, finances, ministries, child bearing, marriages, hearing God and serving Him , and so on).

Appendix C

BY THE AUTHOR

Foundation For Healing is an essential guide to healing the body, soul and spirit, and is the first volume in the Kingdom Medicine Series. It is for those who are new or involved in the healing ministry, and provides a foundation to minister to others in the area of healing, including: *Hearing God; Spiritual and Emotional Roots to Sickness and Disease; Blockages to Healing; Staying Healed; Deliverance Guidelines, and Understanding the Spirit, Soul and Body.* This book aims to encourage and empower the body of Christ to minister to one another, so healing may become the norm in everyone's life.

Divine Heart Surgery is a follow on from *Healing Tools* in the Kingdom Medicine Series. It is a more advanced way to minister healing to the traumatised areas and requires coming into God's Presence to create a safe place to go deeper in the wounded areas of the heart. As we minister in His Presence, we have the privilege of seeing what He does, as He delicately heals and restores the wounded and traumatised areas. It has advanced tools including: *Accessing the Courts of Heaven, Rescue Operations,* and *Uniting the Mind, Will & Emotions.*

HEALING TOOLS

Into His Chambers is based on a vision of the heart that invites the reader to come deeper into the heart of God, by encountering His chambers of *Belonging, Identity, Suffering Heart of Christ* and *Anointing*. It is full of revelatory insight to draw your heart deeper into the heart of God, and this includes understanding the power of His grace and the cross, discovering the full measure of sonship, and a hunger for His Glory-Presence.

At the peak of her medical career, Angela had a call on her life to work amongst the poor in Africa. What she didn't know was that God was going to derail her and take her down an unfamiliar path. As she obeyed God's call, she discovered another realm to sickness and disease; a realm that wasn't found in medical textbooks. Instead she received "on the job training" from the Great Physician Himself. This book combines faith with medicine, the supernatural with the natural and the physical with the emotional and spiritual, as you read the powerful testimonies and teachings on how to heal the sick, God's way!

All books are available on *Amazon* and other online stores.

HEALING TOOLS

Appendix D
ABOUT THE AUTHOR

Angela Walker qualified as a doctor at Liverpool Medical School in 1991 and pursued a career in Paediatrics and Child Health at the London teaching hospitals. She furthered her studies by taking a master's degree in Clinical Paediatrics, followed by a diploma in Tropical Medicine and Hygiene. After this she served with Voluntary Services Oversees as a Paediatric lecturer for eighteen months in Uganda.

Shortly after becoming a consultant in 2004 she went on to study at All Nations Bible College in Hertfordshire. Following this, she served with Iris Global for seven years on the mission fields in Mozambique and South Sudan, where she practiced Kingdom Medicine. During this time she discovered there could be spiritual and emotional roots to sickness and disease, and this prompted her to write her first book, 'Healing God's Way'.

She is an inspirational teacher, trainer and pioneer with a passion to see hearts restored, lives transformed and God's Kingdom advance across the nations. She is the founder and director of THEO Ministries.

For further copies of her books, invitations to speak or any other enquiries please visit the web or email:

www.theoministries.com
info@theoministries.com

Printed in Great Britain
by Amazon